SHORT ROW

knits

SHORT ROW

knits

a master workshop with 20 learn-as-you-knit projects

CAROL FELLER

POTTER
CRAFT

New York

All rights reserved.
Published in the United States by Potter Craft, an
imprint of the Crown Publishing Group, a division
of Penguin Random House LLC, New York.
www.crownpublishing.com
www.pottercraft.com

POTTER CRAFT and colophon are registered
trademarks of Penguin Random House, LLC.

Library of Congress Cataloging-in-Publication Data
is available upon request.

ISBN 978-0-8041-8634-6
eBook ISBN 978-0-8041-8635-3

Printed in China

Text design by La Tricia Watford
Photographs by Joseph Feller
Charts and schematics by Carol and Caelen Feller
Technical editing by Heather Murray
Jacket design by La Tricia Watford
Jacket photographs by Joseph Feller

10 9 8 7 6 5 4 3 2 1

First Edition

CONTENTS

INTRODUCTION

Short rows are one of my favorite knitting techniques. Simply by turning your work before the end of a row, you can create truly magical results. Imagine shaping your knitting to fit your own curves. Or working a lace shawl that never changes stitch count. Or customizing existing patterns to make them exactly right for you!

Have you ever avoided a pattern when you saw that it included short rows? You aren't alone! Over the years I have taught many knitters how to knit short rows, both in person and through my online Craftsy class. Some had already tried short rows but were unhappy with the results because they looked sloppy and weren't well hidden. Others were hesitant to give short rows a try because they thought they were too advanced.

But in my experience, once short rows are explained in logical steps, most knitters pick up the techniques very quickly. My favorite part of teaching short rows is when students have that "Eureka!" moment, when they suddenly get how short rows work. Working through each step methodically, most students learn the basic concepts quickly and are creating neat, nearly invisible short rows within a few hours. Once they do, it opens up a whole new range of possibilities in their knitting. I hope this book does the same for your short rows!

My goal is to demystify short rows so that you are comfortable with the basic idea and to teach you several different ways to create them so you can find the method that best suits you. But more important, I want you to understand that short rows are a powerful and versatile tool. They are powerful because you can use them to create shapes, curves, and extra length in your knitting without ever changing your stitch count.

This is important, because it means that you can easily add short rows to existing patterns without making any other changes. And they are amazingly versatile. In this book you'll learn how to create a variety of two-dimensional shapes, and also how to use short rows to transform a two-dimensional surface into a three-dimensional form. You'll learn how to use short rows to create innovative accessories and to add shoulder shaping, sleeve caps, bust darts, hems, and other elements to garments.

I hope that you will enjoy this book as a tutorial and workbook to master the methods and techniques, and also as an inspiring pattern book with twenty beautiful yet wearable projects. I want you to put theory into practice and learn through experience. Every pattern in this book uses short rows to demonstrate a technique or application so that you have a concrete example in which to perfect your short rows. If you are like me, you have many pristine knitting books tucked away on your shelf, and a select few well-worn knitting books that are always close at hand. I'm hoping this book ends up in the second category for you and inspires you to come back over and over to explore this magical technique and apply these ideas to your current and future works in progress.

HAPPY KNITTING!

short row

TECHNIQUES

In this chapter you will learn several popular methods for creating short rows and experiment with a number of variations. I highly recommend creating the sample swatch with each method so that you are familiar with all of them and can make an informed choice when knitting, as you will no doubt find you favor one or two of the methods over others. After the tutorials and swatch patterns, you'll find patterns for several clever accessories and a cardigan to help you practice your new skills.

Four Short Row Methods

Simply put, short rows are the result of turning your work before you get to the end of the row (or round) and working in the other direction. Simple, right? But what makes short rows sometimes a little tricky in practice—and where most people get tripped up—is knowing what to do *after* the short row is created.

This is because when you turn your work, you create a gap, and if you don't use a method to close that gap, you will have a slight hole and a loose stitch in your work at that location. So the essence of short rows is mastering different methods that have been designed to "close the gap."

In this section, I will show you several different methods for working short rows. For each method I give directions for a swatch to knit and keep for future reference. Make sure to label them and maybe even add your own notes. Each short row swatch has three turns on each side; you can even work all of the short row swatches one on top of each other if you don't bind off before you begin the next swatch.

Note that, for now, I am only describing working short rows in stockinette stitch (knit on the right side and purl on the wrong side) as this is the easiest fabric in which to hide short rows. Other fabric types are discussed in the next section (Beyond the Basics, page 21).

Method 1: Wrap and Turn (W&T)

With the wrap-and-turn short row method, every time you turn your work you wrap a loop of yarn around the next stitch. This loop of yarn is then used to "close" the short row gap when you are finished working your short rows. There are two methods of closing the short row gap in this way: the standard "w&t" method and my alternative.

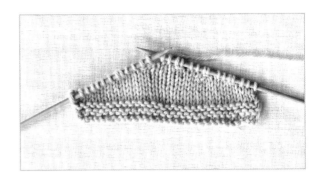

wrap-and-turn swatch instructions

Cast on 28 stitches.

Work 4 rows in garter stitch. Work 4 rows in stockinette stitch.

Short Row 1 (RS): K24, w&t.

Short Row 2 (WS): P20, w&t.

Short Row 3 (RS): K16, w&t.

Short Row 4 (WS): P12, w&t.

Short Row 5 (RS): K8, w&t.

Short Row 6 (WS): P4, w&t.

Next Row (RS): Knit to end of row, picking up all wraps and knitting them with the stitch they wrap.

Next Row (WS): Purl to end of row, picking up all wraps and purling them with the stitch they wrap.

To finish, you can either work 4 rows in garter stitch and bind off or, alternatively, work 1 row of reverse stockinette stitch to mark a division and continue working the other short row techniques with the same swatch.

wrap-and-turn tutorial

On a knit row

Knit to the turning point and slip the next stitch from left to right needle purlwise.

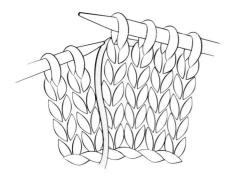

Pass yarn from back to front of work and slip stitch back from right to left needle.

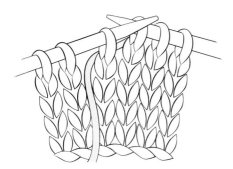

Turn your work to purl side, passing yarn from back to front of work. When you work the next stitch, take care to pull yarn snugly.

On a purl row

Purl to the turning point and slip the next stitch from left to right needle purlwise.

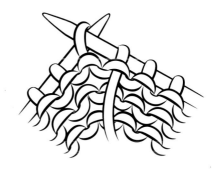

Pass yarn from front to back of work and slip stitch back from right to left needle.

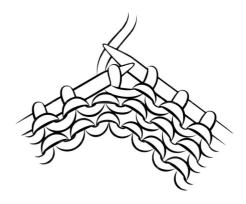

Turn your work to knit side, passing yarn from front to back of work.

When you come to a wrapped stitch in subsequent rows, you may choose one of the following two ways to close the gap.

on subsequent rows—the standard method

For knit stitches

Lift the wrap with the right needle from the right side, lifting from bottom to top of the wrap.

With wrap still on right needle, insert right needle into front of wrapped stitch and knit the wrap together with the stitch.

For purl stitches

Lift the wrap with right needle from the right side of the work, lifting from bottom to top of the wrap, and sit it on the left needle. (Shown from wrong side of work below.)

Purl the wrap together with the stitch that was wrapped.

on subsequent rows—the alternative method

When I come to a wrapped stitch in subsequent rows, rather than using the standard method above, I detach the wrap from the stitch and place it behind the stitch to be worked so that it is completely hidden.

For knit stitches

Lift the wrap with the right needle from the right side of the work, lifting from bottom to top of the wrap. With wrap still on right needle, put right needle through next stitch on left needle knitwise.

Slip both stitches onto right needle and lift wrap over stitch it is wrapping so that wrap sits on other side of stitch.

Knit the stitch and wrap together.

For purl stitches

Lift the wrap with right needle from the right side of the work, lifting from bottom to top of the wrap as for standard method.

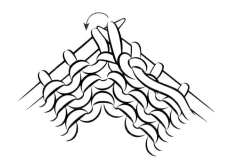

Lift wrap over stitch it wraps and place it behind stitch on left needle.

Purl the wrap together with the stitch that was wrapped as for the standard wrap-and-turn method (see page 12).

(see page 12)

Method 2: Japanese Short Rows

With the Japanese short row method, every time you turn your work you put a safety pin or other marker around the yarn. The loop of yarn that is held by the marker is then used to "close" the short row gap in the same way that the wrap did in the wrap-and-turn method. I have used safety pins for the ease of description here, but a wide variety of things can be used, including lockable stitch markers, bobby pins, or even long scraps of yarn. In fact, if you are working several Japanese short rows next to each other, you can use a single long strand of yarn for all of them.

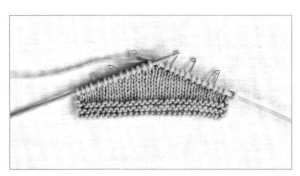

Japanese short rows swatch instructions

Cast on 28 stitches.

Work 4 rows in garter stitch. Work 4 rows in stockinette stitch.

Short Row 1 (RS): K24, turn.

Short Row 2 (WS): Slip stitch purlwise, place safety pin around yarn, p19, turn.

Short Row 3 (RS): Slip stitch purlwise, place safety pin around yarn, k15, turn.

Short Row 4 (WS): Slip stitch purlwise, place safety pin around yarn, p11, turn.

Short Row 5 (RS): Slip stitch purlwise, place safety pin around yarn, k7, turn.

Short Row 6 (WS): Slip stitch purlwise, place safety pin around yarn, p3, turn.

Next Row (RS): Slip stitch purlwise, place safety pin around yarn, knit to end of row, working all yarn loops held on safety pins with the corresponding stitch.

Next Row (WS): Purl to end of row, working all yarn loops held on safety pins with the corresponding stitch.

To finish, you can either work 4 rows in garter stitch and bind off or, alternatively, work 1 row of reverse stockinette stitch to mark a division and continue working the other short row techniques with the same swatch.

Japanese short rows tutorial

On a knit row

Knit to the turning point, turn work.

Slip stitch purlwise, with yarn in front, from the left to the right needle and attach safety pin around working yarn (the pin will hang on the wrong side of the work, facing you).

On a purl row

Purl to the turning point, turn work.

Slip stitch purlwise, with yarn in back, from the left to the right needle, and attach pin around working yarn; the pin will hang on the wrong side of the work, away from you.

on subsequent rows

For knit stitches

Work to the gap; pin is attached to the yarn loop behind your right needle.

Pull pin up to lift the yarn loop and place the loop on left needle. Remove pin.

Knit yarn loop and next stitch together.

For purl stitches

Purl to the gap; pin will be attached to yarn loop under your right needle.

Slip next stitch purlwise from left to right needle.

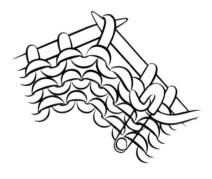

Pull pin up to lift the yarn loop and place loop on left needle. Remove pin.

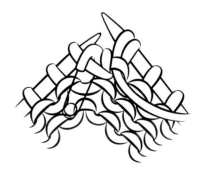

Slip stitch back from right to left needle.

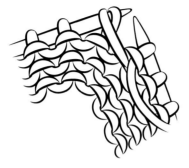

Purl stitch together with yarn loop.

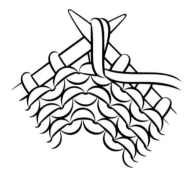

Method 3: Yarn-Over Short Rows

With this method, every time you turn your work you create a yarn over on your needle. This is effectively the same as the wrap from the wrap-and-turn method except that the "wrap" is being held on your needle as a yarn over or yarn loop. You use this yarn over to close the short row gap in the same way that the wrap did for the wrap-and-turn method. With yarn-over short rows, you need to take care with your stitch counting. The yarn over creates a double stitch that *must be counted as only 1 stitch*.

yarn-over short rows swatch instructions

Cast on 28 stitches.

Work 4 rows in garter stitch. Work 4 rows in stockinette stitch.

Short Row 1 (RS): K24, turn.

Short Row 2 (WS): Yo, p20, turn.

Short Row 3 (RS): Yo, k16, turn.

Short Row 4 (WS): Yo, p12, turn.

Short Row 5 (RS): Yo, k8, turn.

Short Row 6 (WS): Yo, p4, turn.

Next Row (RS): Yo, knit to end of row, working all yarn overs with the corresponding stitch.

Next Row (WS): Purl to end of row, working all yarn overs with the corresponding stitch.

To finish, you can either work 4 rows in garter stitch and bind off or, alternatively, work 1 row of reverse stockinette stitch to mark a division and continue working the other short row techniques with the same swatch.

yarn-over short rows tutorial

On a knit row

Knit to turning point, turn work.

Bring the yarn to the back of your work and begin working a purl row. As the yarn is brought to front of the work for the first purl stitch, you will create a yarn-over loop in front of the first stitch. It looks like a double stitch.

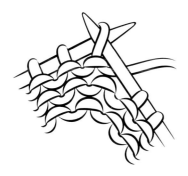

On a purl row

Purl to turning point, turn work.

Bring the yarn to the front of your work and begin working a knit row. As the yarn is brought to back of work for the first knit stitch, you will create a yarn-over loop in front of the first stitch.

here's what to do when you come to a "double stitch" in subsequent rows

For knit stitches

Work to the double stitch; the second stitch of this is the yarn over that you will use to close the gap.

Knit first stitch.

Remount the yarn over correctly.

Knit 2 stitches together.

For purl stitches

Work to the double stitch; the second stitch of this is the yarn over that you will use to close the gap. Purl the first stitch.

Slip 2 stitches knitwise, one at a time, from left to right needle.

Move these 2 stitches back to the left needle and purl both stitches together through the back loop (this is an ssp).

Method 4: German Short Rows

The German short row method is quite different from the other three. Each of the other methods uses a loop of yarn (held in different ways) to close the gap created when you turn your work. However, with the German method, you are effectively pulling up the stitch from the row below when you turn to minimize the impact of the turn. As with the yarn-over method, you need to take care when counting stitches, as each "double stitch" *is counted as a single stitch.*

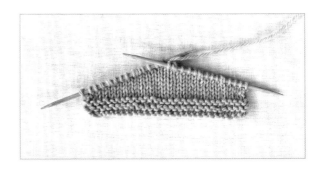

German short rows swatch instructions

Cast on 28 stitches.

Work 4 rows in garter stitch. Work 4 rows in stockinette stitch.

Short Row 1 (RS): K24, turn.

Short Row 2 (WS): Slip stitch purlwise, pull yarn over needle, p19, turn.

Short Row 3 (RS): Slip stitch purlwise, pull yarn over needle, k15, turn.

Short Row 4 (WS): Slip stitch purlwise, pull yarn over needle, p11, turn.

Short Row 5 (RS): Slip stitch purlwise, pull yarn over needle, k7, turn.

Short Row 6 (WS): Slip stitch purlwise, pull yarn over needle, p3, turn.

Next Row (RS): Slip stitch purlwise, pull yarn over needle, knit to end of row, working all double stitches as single stitches.

Next Row (WS): Purl to end of row, working all double stitches as single stitches.

To finish, you can either work 4 rows in garter stitch and bind off or, alternatively, work 1 row of reverse stockinette stitch to mark a division and continue working the other short row techniques with the same swatch.

German short rows tutorial

On a knit row

Knit to the turning point, turn work.

Slip stitch purlwise, with yarn in front, from the left to the right needle. Pull the working yarn up and over the right needle. This creates a double stitch by pulling up the stitch from the row below.

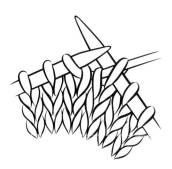

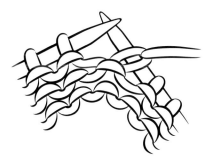

Bring the yarn between the needles to the front of the work to begin working the purl row. Take care that you do not lose your double stitch.

On a purl row

Purl to the turning point, turn work.

Slip stitch purlwise, with yarn in front, from the left to the right needle. Pull the working yarn up and over the right needle. This creates a double stitch by pulling up the stitch from the row below.

here's what to do when you come to a "double stitch" in subsequent rows

For knit stitches

Knit the double stitch together as though it were 1 stitch.

For purl stitches

Purl the double stitch together as though it were 1 stitch.

Which Method Is Best?

This is a very subjective question! I teach a wide range of short row techniques, as I find that every knitter is unique, and one style does not suit all.

Different short row techniques are more effective for different projects. For example, if I'm working with a heavier-weight yarn that is knit at a tighter gauge, I can use any technique that's fast for me to work, as the short rows will all be well hidden in the knitting. On the other hand, if I'm using a lace-weight yarn at a loose gauge, the fabric becomes very transparent. For this type of knitting, I prefer to use the technique that creates the most-invisible short rows, which, for me, tends to be Japanese short rows. Finally, for garter stitch I find that German short rows win hands down every time; they're fast to work and blend in beautifully.

To help you choose the best short row technique for specific projects, I've included a short row suggestion for each pattern in this book. Please do remember that it's just a suggestion, and you can substitute a different technique if you prefer. Do pay attention in the pattern instructions though, as the description of how to work your short rows will be slightly different for each technique.

short row method comparison

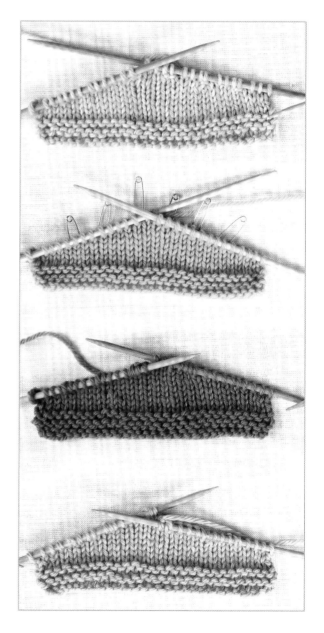

HELPFUL REMINDERS

- When working with yarn-over and German short rows, remember *not* to include the extra stitch in your stitch count.
- For several Japanese short rows worked in a row, try using a long strand of yarn (rather than pins or markers) for all of the short rows yarn loops; it makes them very fast to work!
- If you are substituting different short row techniques in a pattern, make sure you put them in the correct position. If you look at the short row comparision photo, you can see how each short row type looks a little different. If a pattern is written for wrap-and-turn method and you want to use Japanese, every time it says to "work to the previous wrapped stitch," you will need to work as far as the gap.

As you can see from the photo opposite, of all four methods, they look a little different when they are worked. With the wrap-and-turn technique, you have the wrap outside the gap. With Japanese short rows, you have the safety pin hanging on the wrong side of the work inside the gap. For yarn overs, you have a double stitch created by the yarn over that sits inside the gap. The German method also creates a double stitch inside the gap. It is important to notice these differences, as they can have an impact on your stitch count if you are substituting a different type of short row method in a pattern.

Beyond the Basics

Previously, we practiced short rows in stockinette stitch, the easiest fabric in which to work—and also to hide— short rows. But you will not always be knitting stockinette stitch; chances are you will be using a wide variety of stitches and textures. In this section we'll look at other fabrics suitable for short rows, so that you can extend beyond basic stockinette.

working short rows in garter stitch

It can be fairly easy to hide short rows in garter stitch, as the bumpy nature of the fabric provides a camouflage for the wraps. If you only have a few short rows in garter stitch, you can use the wrap-and-turn method without picking up the wraps. It can leave a few distorted stitches, but it's not very noticeable.

If you are working a greater number of short rows in garter stitch, I recommend using German short rows. They blend smoothly into the fabric and are very quick to work.

German short rows in garter stitch tutorial

Knit to the turning point, turn work.

Slip stitch purlwise, with yarn in front, from the left to the right needle. Pull the working yarn up and over the right needle. This creates a double stitch by pulling up the stitch from the row below.

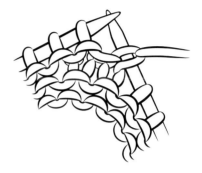

When you come to a double stitch in subsequent rows, knit the double stitch together as though it were 1 stitch.

working short rows in reverse stockinette stitch

When you are working in reverse stockinette stitch, the method is the reverse of standard stockinette. On the right side of your work you will have purl stitches, and on the wrong side you will have knit. I will show you how to work short rows in reverse stockinette stitch using the wrap-and-turn method, but you can use the theory and also apply it to the Japanese method. Use the same basic idea as for stockinette (you use a wrap to close the gap), but this time you will be keeping the wrap on the wrong (knit) side of the fabric so it isn't seen from the right (purl) side. On the front of the fabric there will be 2 loops visible in the stitch, as though you worked 2 stitches together.

wrap and turn
in reverse stockinette stitch tutorial

To create the wraps, work as for the stockinette stitch as shown (see page 11), but purl is right side and knit is wrong side.

on subsequent rows

For knit stitches

Lift the wrap with right needle from the right (purl) side of the work, lifting from bottom to top of the wrap.
Lift wrap over stitch it wraps, and place it behind stitch on left needle.

Knit the wrap together with the stitch that was wrapped.

For purl stitches

Lift the wrap with the right needle from the right (purl) side of the work, lifting from bottom to top of the wrap.
With wrap still on right needle, put right needle through next stitch on left needle knitwise.

Slip both stitches onto right needle and lift wrap over stitch it is wrapping so that wrap sits on other side of stitch.

Slip both wrap and stitch from right to left needle knitwise and purl them together.

working short rows in the round

When you work short rows in a fabric that is being worked in the round, you are still working the short rows back and forth in rows. However, when the short rows are finished, you will begin working in the round again, and the short rows that you created on the right-hand end (when you turned after a wrong-side row) will be joined on the right side. These are going to look a little different, as the wrap is on a different side of the stitch. I am showing them worked using the wrap-and-turn method, but you could try them with the Japanese method instead. With the Japanese method, you may find that the wrap becomes a little tight and distorts the stitch. The yarn-over method also works well in the round.

wrap and turn in the round tutorial

To create the wraps, work as for the stockinette stitch as shown (see page 11).

on subsequent rounds

Lift the wrap with the right needle from the front, lifting from bottom to top of the wrap. With wrap still on right needle, put right needle through next stitch on left needle knitwise.

Slip both stitches onto right needle and lift wrap over stitch it is wrapping, so that wrap sits on other side of stitch.

Knit the stitch and wrap together.

working with pattern stitches

Now that you know how to work short rows with some basic stitches, you may also wish to apply the technique to some more complex patterns. Sometimes this can be done, but take care not to work partial pattern repeats. Consider how it will look, and if you can blend the short rows into the pattern, then it will work. Ideally, if you chart or swatch the short rows before you work to see how it fits the pattern, you won't have any surprises.

If you are working short rows in a pattern that has cable or lace panels, try to work the short rows outside the pattern panel so that you do not interrupt the more complex design. If the pattern you are working has several panels of a chart, but you are only working short rows across one panel, then you should ensure that your short rows are a full pattern repeat. This way, when you begin working the complete piece again, all panels of your pattern will continue to line up.

If you are knitting a piece that has an all-over lace or cable pattern, I would advise against using short rows. It can be done, but it is very tricky!

skill level

Most of the projects in this book are given an intermediate skill level. The Craft Yarn Council (CYC) considers short rows an experienced skill, but I think that with the information given in this book, intermediate knitters should be very comfortable tackling them.

Sapoa
BRAIDED BAG

Knitting this bag from the bottom up, short rows are used to create the curved edges at the bottom of the bag. Plaited cables at the top draw the bag edges in, and they continue on to form the I-cord handles. This project is an ideal first short row project. Try out your wrap-and-turn short rows at the start of the work and then breeze through the rest of the bag in the round!

Skill Level Intermediate

Size One Size

Finished Measurements
Width at base: 13½" (34.5cm)
Bag height (omitting handles and bottom curve):
9¾" (24.5cm)
Bag depth: 2¾" (7cm)

Materials
YARN
2 skeins Malabrigo Rios, 100% superwash merino, 3.5 oz (100g), 210 yds (192m), in Sunset (96) (**4**) medium

NEEDLES & NOTIONS
1 US size 7 (4.5mm) circular needle, 24" (61cm) long
Set of US size 7 (4.5mm) double-pointed needles
Adjust needle size as necessary to achieve gauge.
US size G-6 (4mm) crochet hook for provisional cast-on

Waste yarn for provisional cast-on
Stitch holders or second needle
Stitch markers
Cable needle
Tapestry needle

Gauge
20 stitches and 28 rows = 4" (10cm) in stockinette stitch
Braided cable measures 1½" (3.8cm) across

Short Row Method Used
Wrap and Turn (page 10)

Techniques
For other techniques used in the pattern, please refer to General Techniques (page 155).

I-CORD
*Knit 3 stitches, slip 3 stitches just worked to the other end of the double-pointed needle and tug yarn snugly; repeat from * until I-cord is desired length.

BRAIDING

With all 3 I-cords facing you, *pass right cord over center cord, then pass left cord over center cord; repeat from * until all of the I-cord is braided.

CABLES

3/3 LC: Slip 3 stitches onto a cable needle and hold at the front of the work. Knit 3 stitches then knit the 3 stitches from the cable needle.

3/3 RC: Slip 3 stitches onto a cable needle and hold at the back of the work. Knit 3 stitches then knit the 3 stitches from the cable needle.

BRAIDED CABLE PATTERN

Rnds 1, 2, 4, 5, 6, and 8: P1, knit to last stitch, p1.

Rnd 3: P1, 3/3 RC, k3, p1.

Rnd 7: P1, k3, 3/3 LC, p1.

Repeat rounds 1–8 for braided cable.

BRAIDED CABLE CHART

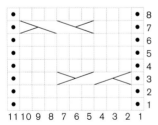

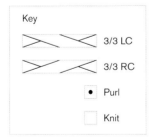

SHORT ROW BASE

With circular needle, cast on 70 stitches using a provisional cast-on.

Next row (WS): Purl.

***Short Row 1 (RS):** K45, w&t.

Short Row 2 (WS): K20, w&t.

Short Row 3 (RS): Knit to previously wrapped stitch, knit wrap with stitch it wraps, k1, w&t.

Short Row 4 (WS): Purl to previously wrapped stitch, purl wrap with stitch it wraps, p1, w&t.

Work short rows 3 and 4 eleven more times.

Knit to end of row, working wrap with the stitch it wraps as you pass it.*

Place all stitches on a holder.

Undo provisional cast-on and place all 70 stitches on the circular needle.

Work in garter stitch for 32 rows (16 "bumps"), ending with a wrong-side row.

Work short rows as above from * to *.

Pick up and knit 18 stitches from side of garter stitch, knit held 70 stitches, pick up and knit 18 stitches from second side of garter stitch, knit 5 stitches, place a marker for start of round—176 stitches.

BODY

Setup Rnd: K60, work braided cable over next 11 stitches, k6, work braided cable, k60, work braided cable, k6, work braided cable.

Continue to work in the pattern established until braided cable measures 9" (23cm) or desired bag depth.

Dec Rnd: *Knit to braided cable, work braided cable, ssk, knit to 2 stitches before braided cable, k2tog, work braided cable; repeat from * once more—172 stitches.

Next rnd: *Purl to braided cable, work braided cable, knit to next braided cable, work braided cable; repeat from * once more.

Work these 2 rounds once more—168 stitches.

Dec Rnd: *Knit to braided cable, work braided cable, ssk, knit to braided cable, work braided cable; repeat from * once more, stopping before final cable stitch—166 stitches.

HANDLES

*Bind off 62 stitches using I-cord bind-off, work braided cable from stitches 2–10, bind off 3 stitches using standard bind-off, work braided cable from stitches 2–10; repeat from * once.

You will now work on the final cable only. Place the other 3 cables onto holders.

Divide every set of 3 stitches onto 3 separate double-pointed needles. Work each set of 3 stitches in I-cord until they measure 12" (30.5cm) or desired length for half the handle length. Place stitches on holders.

Repeat these I-cords for the other 3 cables.

Braid the I-cords from each cable, crossing them to match the braided cable as closely as possible. When the braid is complete, place all 9 stitches on a double-pointed needle to hold in position. Graft I-cords together from the cables at each side of the bag to create a complete braided bag handle and sew the top of the braid together to prevent it from unraveling.

FINISHING

Weave in all loose ends. Block bag to dimensions given. Stuffing the bag with an absorbent material while it dries helps it retain its shape.

frio
CABLED HAT

Knit from the front to the back of the head in one piece, this hat uses short rows to smoothly curve its shape. The ribbed band is worked afterward to ensure a good fit on the head. Japanese short rows are an ideal choice here, as the short rows are worked very close together in a visible location.

Skill Level Intermediate

Sizes

To fit head circumference up to 19¼ (21¼, 23¾)" (49 [54, 60.5]cm)
2" (5cm) negative ease recommended

Finished Measurements

Hat circumference: 17¼ (19¼, 21¾)" (44 [49, 55.5]cm)
Size 19¼" (49cm) modeled with 2" (5cm) of negative ease

Materials

YARN

1 (1, 1) skein Cascade Longwood, 100% merino, 3.53 oz (100g), 191 yd (175m), in Color 11 (**4**) medium

NEEDLES & NOTIONS

1 US size 7 (4.5mm) circular needle, 16" (40.5cm) long
Adjust needle size as necessary to achieve gauge.
US size G-6 (4mm) crochet hook for provisional cast-on
Waste yarn for provisional cast-on
Stitch markers
Safety pins or waste yarn for Japanese short rows
Cable needle
Tapestry needle

Gauge

24 stitches and 30 rows = 4" (10cm) in stockinette stitch, blocked
Cable chart measures 2¼" (5.5cm) wide

Short Row Method Used

Japanese (page 14)

Techniques

For other techniques used in the pattern, please refer to General Techniques (page 155).

CABLES

2/2 RC: Slip 2 stitches onto cable needle, hold to back of work. Knit 2 stitches, knit 2 stitches from cable needle.

2/1 RPC: Slip 1 stitch onto cable needle, hold to back of work. Knit 2 stitches, purl 1 stitch from cable needle.

2/1 LPC: Slip 2 stitches onto cable needle, hold to front of work. Purl 1 stitch, knit 2 stitches from cable needle.

CABLE CHART

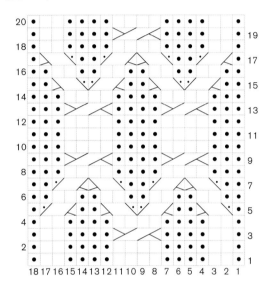

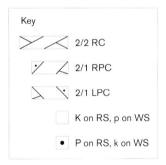

Pattern Notes

When working several Japanese short rows one after another, it can be faster to use a long piece of yarn instead of safety pins, looping the yarn across the working yarn every time you work a short row.

BODY OF HAT

Using provisional cast-on method, cast on 52 (58, 66) stitches.

Note: Written directions for the cable chart are included in the pattern instructions, but you may also use the cable chart for the section between markers below.

Row 1 (RS): K17 (20, 24), place marker (slip this marker after first repeat), p1, k2, p4, k4, p4, k2, p1, place marker (slip this marker after first repeat), knit to end of row.

Row 2 (WS): Purl to marker, slip marker, k1, p2, k4, p4, k4, p2, k1, slip marker, purl to end of row.

Row 3 (RS): Slip stitch, place safety pin, knit to marker, slip marker, p1, k2, p4, 2/2 RC, p4, k2, p1, slip marker, k16 (18, 21), turn work.

Row 4 (WS): Slip stitch, place safety pin, purl to marker, slip marker, k1, p2, k4, p4, k4, p2, k1, slip marker, p16 (18, 21), turn work.

Row 5 (RS): Slip stitch, place safety pin, knit to marker, slip marker, p1, *2/1 LPC, p2, 2/1 RPC; repeat from * once, p1, slip marker, k14 (16, 19), turn work.

Row 6 (WS): Slip stitch, place safety pin, purl to marker, slip marker, *k2, p2; repeat from * 3 more times, k2, slip marker, p14 (16, 19), turn work.

Row 7 (RS): Slip stitch, place safety pin, knit to marker, slip marker, *p2, 2/1 LPC, 2/1 RPC; repeat from * once more, p2, slip marker, k12 (14, 17), turn work.

Row 8 (WS): Slip stitch, place safety pin, purl to marker, slip marker, k3, p4, k4, p4, k3, slip marker, p12 (14, 17), turn work.

Row 9 (RS): Slip stitch, place safety pin, knit to marker, slip marker, p3, 2/2 RC, p4, 2/2 RC, p3, slip marker, k10 (12, 15), turn work.

Row 10 (WS): Slip stitch, place safety pin, purl to marker, slip marker, k3, p4, k4, p4, k3, slip marker, p10 (12, 15), turn work.

Row 11 (RS): Slip stitch, place safety pin, knit to marker, slip marker, p3, k4, p4, k4, p3, slip marker, k8 (10, 13), turn work.

Row 12 (WS): Slip stitch, place safety pin, purl to marker, slip marker, k3, p4, k4, p4, k3, slip marker, p8 (10, 13), turn work.

Row 13 (RS): Slip stitch, place safety pin, knit to marker, slip marker, p3, 2/2 RC, p4, 2/2 RC, p3, slip marker, k6 (8, 11), turn work.

Row 14 (WS): Slip stitch, place safety pin, purl to marker, slip marker, k3, p4, k4, p4, k3, slip marker, p6 (8, 11), turn work.

Row 15 (RS): Slip stitch, place safety pin, knit to marker, slip marker, *P2, 2/1 RPC, 2/1 LPC; repeat from * once more, p2, slip marker, k4 (6, 9), turn work.

Row 16 (WS): Slip stitch, place safety pin, purl to marker, slip marker, *k2, p2; repeat from * 3 more times, k2, slip marker, p4 (6, 9), turn work.

Row 17 (RS): Slip stitch, place safety pin, knit to marker, slip marker, p1, *2/1 RPC, p2, 2/1 LPC; repeat from * once more, p1, slip marker, k2 (4, 6), turn work.

Row 18 (WS): Slip stitch, place safety pin, purl to marker, slip marker, k1, p2, k4, p4, k4, p2, k1, slip marker, p2 (4, 6), turn work.

Row 19 (RS): Slip stitch, place safety pin, knit to marker, slip marker, p1, k2, p4, 2/2 RC, p4, k2, p1, slip marker, k1 (2, 3), turn work.

Row 20 (WS): Slip stitch, place safety pin, purl to marker, slip marker, k1, p2, k4, p4, k4, p2, k1, slip marker, p1 (2, 3), turn work.

Repeat rows 1–20 as above 3 (3, 4) more times. Take care to work each of the yarn loops with the corresponding stitch when working rows 1 and 2 after the first repeat.

Work rows 1 and 2 once more, working all remaining yarn loops with the corresponding stitches.

EDGING

*K1, p1; repeat from * to end of row, pick up and knit 4 stitches down side of work, undo provisional cast-on, placing resultant 52 (58, 66) stitches on the needle, *k1, p1; repeat from * to end of row, pick up and knit 4 stitches down side of work. Join to work in the round, placing marker for start of round—112 (124, 140) stitches.

Ribbing Rnd: *K1, p1; repeat from * to end of round.

Work ribbing rnd until edging measures 1¾ (2, 2)" (4.5 [5, 5]cm) or desired length.

Bind off all stitches in pattern.

FINISHING

Weave in all loose ends. Block hat, taking care to shape it with a bowl or other hat-shaped form.

chirripo
SHORT ROW BALL

This ball is the ideal way to improve your German short row technique and create a unique finished piece. It is knit from side to side in a series of short row wedges that allow you to create a three-dimensional shape using only short rows. Short rows are worked in the garter stitch section of the ball, making the German technique perfect to use—it's fast and nearly invisible!

Skill Level Intermediate

Size One size

Measurements
Ball circumference: 17½" (44.5cm)

Materials

YARN

1 skein Malabrigo Sock, 100% merino, 3.5 oz (100g), 440 yds (402m), in Impressionist Sky (806) ❶ super fine

NEEDLES & NOTIONS
1 set of US size 2 (2.75mm) straight needles
Adjust needle size as necessary to achieve gauge.
US size C-2 (2.75mm) crochet hook for provisional cast-on
Waste yarn for provisional cast-on
Stitch markers
Tapestry needle
Stuffing

Gauge
28 stitches and 45 rows = 4" (10cm) in stockinette stitch, blocked

Short Row Method Used
German (page 18)

Techniques
For other techniques used in the pattern, please refer to General Techniques (page 155).

Pattern Notes
This pattern uses the German method of short rows, which is the fastest option for garter stitch, and will be neatly hidden in this stitch pattern. You can try upsizing this ball by using a chunky yarn with larger needles. It is even possible to make it large enough to use as a footstool!

WEDGE SETUP

Using provisional cast-on, cast on 50 stitches with waste yarn.

With working yarn, knit all stitches.

SHORT ROW WEDGE

Short Row 1 (RS): Slip stitch knitwise, k47, turn work.

Short Row 2 (WS): Slip stitch purlwise with yarn at front of work, pull working yarn up and over the needle, creating a double stitch, k16, p12, k17, turn work.

Short Row 3 (RS): Slip stitch, pull yarn over needle, k43, turn work.

Short Row 4 (WS): Slip stitch, pull yarn over needle, k12, p16, k13, turn work.

Short Row 5 (RS): Slip stitch, pull yarn over needle, k39, turn work.

Short Row 6 (WS): Slip stitch, pull yarn over needle, k7, p22, k8, turn work.

Short Row 7 (RS): Slip stitch, pull yarn over needle, k35, turn work.

Short Row 8 (WS): Slip stitch, pull yarn over needle, k3, p26, k4, turn work.

Short Row 9 (RS): Slip stitch, pull yarn over needle, k31, turn work.

Short Row 10 (WS): Slip stitch, pull yarn over needle, k7, p14, k8, turn work.

Short Row 11 (RS): Slip stitch, pull yarn over needle, k27, turn work.

Short Row 12 (WS): Slip stitch, pull yarn over needle, k3, p18, k4, turn work.

Short Row 13 (RS): Slip stitch, pull yarn over needle, k23, turn work.

Short Row 14 (WS): Slip stitch, pull yarn over needle, k3, p14, k4, turn work.

Short Row 15 (RS): Slip stitch, pull yarn over needle, k19, turn work.

Short Row 16 (WS): Slip stitch, pull yarn over needle, k2, p12, k3, turn work.

Short Row 17 (RS): Slip stitch, pull yarn over needle, k15, turn work.

Short Row 18 (WS): Slip stitch, pull yarn over needle, k1, p10, k2, turn work.

Short Row 19 (RS): Slip stitch, pull yarn over needle, knit to end of row.

Short Row 20 (WS): Slip stitch knitwise, knit to end of row.

Work short rows 1–20 nine more times. Break yarn, leaving a tail long enough to graft all 50 stitches.

FINISHING

Undo the provisional cast-on, placing all 50 stitches on a second needle.

With start and end of ball held together and the right side facing you, graft 40 stitches together and partially stuff the ball. Graft the final 10 stitches and finish stuffing the ball. With the remaining yarn tail, pull the tapestry needle through the slipped selvedge stitches around the end and draw the small hole at the end together. Repeat this at the other side of the ball. Weave in all loose ends.

Shape the ball gently to achieve the shape you want. Spray with water or steam to block gently.

toro

CARDI WITH SHAWL COLLAR

Elegant and practical, a shawl collar keeps you warm and looks great! This cardigan is knit in one piece from the bottom up; the body uses a beautiful acorn lace pattern that flows smoothly into the ribbed yoke. Short rows are used afterward to shape the ribbed shawl collar. As the collar is worked in ribbing, you will be knitting short rows on reverse stockinette stitch as well as stockinette.

Skill Level Intermediate

Sizes and Finished Measurements

To Fit Bust Circumference (up to)	31" (79cm)	35½" (90cm)	40¼" (102cm)	44¾" (113.5cm)	49¼" (125cm)	53½" (136cm)	58½" (149cm)
Finished Bust Circumference (buttoned)	32" (81cm)	36½" (92.5cm)	41¼" (105cm)	45¾" (116cm)	50¼" (127.5cm)	54½" (138cm)	59½" (151cm)
Length	21¾" (55.5cm)	22¼" (56.5cm)	23" (58.5cm)	23¾" (60cm)	24¼" (61.5cm)	24¾" (63cm)	25¼" (64cm)

Size 36½" (92.5cm) modeled with 2" (5cm) of positive ease

Materials

YARN

5 (5, 6, 7, 7, 8, 8) skeins Lorna's Laces Shepherd Worsted, 100% superwash merino wool, 4 oz (113g), 225 yds (206m), in Cranberry (45ns) [4] medium

NEEDLES & NOTIONS

1 US size 8 (5mm) circular needle, 40" (101.5cm) long (or longer for larger cardigan size)
1 set US size 8 (5mm) double-pointed needles
Adjust needle size as necessary to achieve gauge.
Stitch markers
Waste yarn
Stitch holders

(continues)

NEEDLES & NOTIONS (continued)

Tapestry needle

6 buttons, ¾" (2cm) diameter

Gauge

20 stitches and 28 rows = 4" (10cm) in stockinette stitch, blocked

21 stitches and 28 rows = 4" (10 cm) in acorn lace pattern and ribbing pattern, blocked

Short Row Method Used

Wrap and Turn (page 10)

Techniques

For other techniques used in the pattern, please refer to General Techniques (page 155).

SINGLE-ROW BUTTONHOLE

Work to buttonhole position, slip stitch with yarn in front, slip next stitch with yarn in back, pass first slipped stitch over the newly slipped stitch, *slip stitch, pass the previously slipped stitch over the newly slipped stitch; repeat from * once, then move the resulting stitch back onto left needle.

Turn work; cast on 4 stitches using cable cast-on method. Turn work again; slip stitch from left to right needle and pass the last cast-on stitch over it. Continue in pattern to next buttonhole.

Note: All stitches are slipped purlwise.

RIBBING PATTERN

Row 1 (RS): *K3, p3; repeat from * to end of row.

Row 2 (WS): *K3, p3; repeat from * to end of row.

Repeat Rows 1 and 2 for the ribbing pattern.

ACORN LACE PATTERN

Rows 1, 2, 3, and 4: *K3, p3; repeat from * to end.

Row 5 (RS): *Yo, k3tog, yo, k3; repeat from * to end.

Row 6 (WS): Purl all stitches.

Rows 7 and 8: *P3, k3; repeat from * to end.

Row 9 (RS): *K3, yo, k3tog, yo; repeat from * to end.

Row 10 (WS): Purl all stitches.

Repeat rows 1–10 for acorn lace pattern.

ACORN LACE CHART

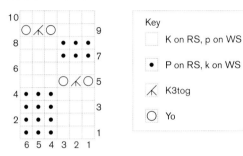

BODY

With circular needle, cast on 148 (172, 196, 220, 244, 268, 292) stitches.

Next row (RS): K2, work in ribbing pattern to last 2 stitches, k2.

Next row (WS): P2, work in ribbing pattern to last 2 stitches, p2.

Continue to work in pattern established until the work measures 3" (7.5cm), ending with a wrong-side row.

Next row (RS): K2, work in acorn lace pattern to last 2 stitches, k2.

Next row (WS): P2, work in acorn lace pattern to last 2 stitches, p2.

Continue to work in pattern established until 8 complete repeats of the acorn lace pattern have been worked. Work should measure 14½" (37cm) from cast-on edge.

Set stitches aside but do not break the yarn.

SLEEVES

Using double-pointed needles, cast on 42 (42, 48, 48, 48, 48, 54) stitches, place marker for start of round and join to work in the round.

Rib Rnd: *K3, p3; repeat from * to end of round.

Work rib rnd until work measures 3" (7.5cm).

Work in stockinette stitch for 10 (9, 9, 8, 6, 5, 5) rounds.

Inc Rnd: K1, M1L, knit to last stitch, M1R, k1—2 stitches increased.

Repeat these 11 (10, 10, 9, 7, 6, 6) rounds 7 (8, 8, 10, 14, 16, 15) more times—58 (60, 66, 70, 78, 82, 86) stitches.

Work even in stockinette stitch until sleeve measures 18 (18½, 18½, 19, 19, 19½, 19½)" (45.5 [47, 47, 48.5, 48.5, 49.5, 49.5]cm) from cast-on or for desired length, ending 2 (5, 7, 9, 12, 15, 17) stitches before the end of round. Place next 4 (10, 14, 18, 24, 30, 34) stitches from start and end of round on waste yarn—54 (50, 52, 52, 54, 52, 52) stitches.

Set stitches aside on holder or waste yarn and break working yarn.

Repeat for second sleeve.

YOKE

Joining Rnd: With body stitches on circular needle and using working yarn attached to body, k2, work in ribbing pattern for 28 (31, 35, 39, 42, 45, 49) stitches, taking care to match knit and purl with acorn lace pattern, slip next 4 (10, 14, 18, 24, 30, 34) stitches onto waste yarn, place marker, k54 (50, 52, 52, 54, 52, 52) sleeve stitches, place marker, work in ribbing pattern for 28 (31, 35, 39, 42, 45, 49) stitches, work 24 stitches in acorn lace pattern, work in ribbing pattern for 28 (31, 35, 39, 42, 45, 49) stitches, slip next 4 (10, 14, 18, 24, 30, 34) stitches onto waste yarn, place marker, k54 (50, 52, 52, 54, 52, 52) sleeve stitches, place marker, work in ribbing pattern for 28 (31, 35, 39, 42, 45, 49) stitches, k2—248 (252, 272, 288, 304, 312, 328) stitches total; 54 (50, 52, 52, 54, 52, 52)

sleeve stitches, 80 (86, 94, 102, 108, 114, 122) back stitches, 30 (33, 37, 41, 44, 47, 51) front stitches.

Work wrong-side row in pattern established.

Body Dec Row (RS): *Work in pattern to 2 stitches before marker, ssk, slip marker, knit to marker, slip marker, k2tog; repeat from * once more, work in pattern to end of row—4 stitches decreased.

Next row (WS): *Work in pattern to 1 stitch before marker, p1, slip marker, purl to marker, slip marker, p1; repeat from * once more, work in pattern to end of row.

Repeat these last 2 rows 0 (1, 2, 3, 4, 5, 6) more times—244 (244, 260, 272, 284, 288, 300) stitches.

Raglan/Neck Dec Row (RS): K1, k2tog, *work in pattern to 2 stitches before marker, ssk, slip marker, k2tog; repeat from * 3 more times, work in pattern to last 3 stitches, ssk, k1—10 stitches decreased.

Next row (WS): *Work in pattern to 1 stitch before marker, p1, slip marker, purl to marker, slip marker, p1; repeat from * once more, work in pattern to end of row.

Work body dec row.

Work wrong-side row.

Repeat these 4 rows (2, 4, 5, 5, 8, 9) more times—244 (202, 190, 188, 200, 162, 160) stitches.

All Sizes

Work raglan/neck dec row.

Work wrong-side row.

Raglan Dec Row (RS): *Work in pattern to 2 stitches before marker, ssk, slip marker, k2tog; repeat from * 3 more times, work in pattern to end of row—8 stitches decreased.

Work wrong-side row.

Repeat these 4 rows 3 (1, 0, 1, 2, 0, 1) more time(s)—172 (166, 172, 152, 146, 144, 124) stitches.

Work raglan dec row.

Work wrong-side row.

Repeat these 2 rows 14 (13, 13, 10, 9, 8, 5) more times—52 (54, 60, 64, 66, 72, 76) stitches total; 8 (8, 10, 10, 10, 12, 12) sleeve stitches, 32 (34, 36, 40, 42, 44, 48) back stitches, 2 front stitches each side.

Break yarn and leave yoke stitches on the needle. Remove all markers.

FINISHING

Collar

With circular needle, starting at the bottom right front of cardigan, with right side facing, pick up and knit 100 (105, 108, 112, 111, 114, 118) stitches to edge of held stitches, place marker, k52 (54, 60, 64, 66, 72, 76) held stitches, place marker, pick up and knit 103 (102, 105, 109, 114, 117, 121) stitches to bottom of left side—255 (261, 273, 285, 291, 303, 315) stitches.

Next row (WS): P3, work in ribbing pattern row 2 to end of row.

Short Rows 1 and 2: Work in pattern to second marker, slip marker, work 2 (3, 3, 3, 3, 4, 4) stitches in pattern, w&t.

Short Rows 3 and 4: Work in pattern to previously wrapped stitch, work 2 (3, 3, 3, 3, 4, 4) stitches in pattern, working wrap with stitch it wraps as you pass, w&t.

Repeat short rows 3 and 4 as above 10 more times.

Work in pattern to the end of the row.

Work 11 more rows in pattern.

Buttonhole Row (RS): Work 2 stitches, *work single-row buttonhole, work 9 stitches; repeat from * 5 more times, work in pattern to the end of the row.

Continue to work in ribbing pattern until work measures 3" (7.5cm) from picked-up stitches. Bind off all stitches loosely in pattern.

Graft 4 (10, 14, 18, 24, 30, 34) stitches from underarm together on each side.

Sew buttons in position opposite buttonholes.

Using tapestry needle, weave in all loose ends. Gently block to dimensions given on schematic.

Note: Schematic does not include shawl collar and button band.

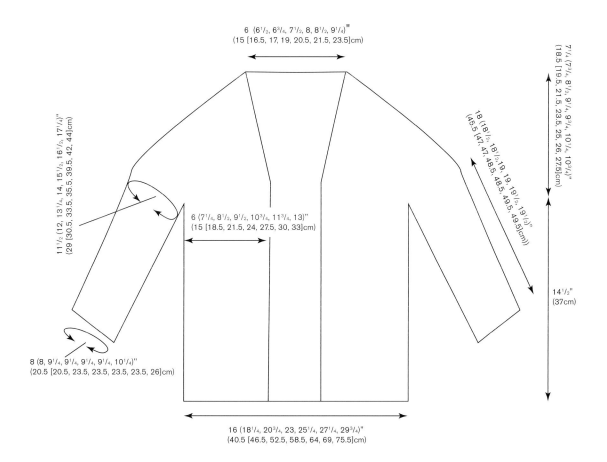

6 (6¹/₂, 6³/₄, 7¹/₂, 8, 8¹/₂, 9¹/₄)"
(15 [16.5, 17, 19, 20.5, 21.5, 23.5]cm)

7¹/₄ (7³/₄, 8¹/₂, 9¹/₄, 9³/₄, 10¹/₄, 10³/₄)"
(18.5 [19.5, 21.5, 23.5, 25, 26, 27.5]cm)

18 (18¹/₂, 18³/₄, 19, 19, 19¹/₂, 19¹/₂)"
(45.5 [47, 47, 48.5, 48.5, 49.5, 49.5]cm))

11¹/₂ (12, 13¹/₄, 14, 15¹/₂, 16¹/₂, 17¹/₄)"
(29 [30.5, 33.5, 35.5, 39.5, 42, 44]cm)

6 (7¹/₄, 8¹/₂, 9¹/₂, 10³/₄, 11³/₄, 13)"
(15 [18.5, 21.5, 24, 27.5, 30, 33]cm)

14¹/₂"
(37cm)

8 (8, 9¹/₄, 9¹/₄, 9¹/₄, 9¹/₄, 10¹/₄)"
(20.5 [20.5, 23.5, 23.5, 23.5, 23.5, 26]cm)

16 (18¹/₄, 20³/₄, 23, 25¹/₄, 27¹/₄, 29³/₄)"
(40.5 [46.5, 52.5, 58.5, 64, 69, 75.5]cm)

short row
SHAPING

Once you know how to create short rows, the next step is to learn
how to apply them to change the shape of your knitting. We'll
start with directional slopes, showing how short rows used only
on one side of your work create a one-sided slope. From there,
we will move onto double slopes and then more complex shapes.
Once you understand how to control your short row shapes, you
can begin adding them to customize your projects. Maybe it will
even be the starting point for your own designs!

Basic Shapes
triangle with a single slope

A short row triangle is created using a series of short rows on either the right or left side, depending on the direction you want for your slope.

left-side slope In the first swatch, short rows are worked every three stitches six times on the right side of the work, and then worked all the way to the end on the wrong-side row. You can see how this creates a slope along the left side of the swatch.

right-side slope In the second swatch, the shaping has been reversed. Short rows are worked every three stitches six times on the wrong-side rows, and the right-side rows are knit to the end.

Using these basic swatches as templates, you can see how you can easily change the shape of your knitting without ever changing your stitch count. You could use this technique in shawls or garments to create asymmetrical shapes, shawls that slope on one side, or a hem that dips on one side.

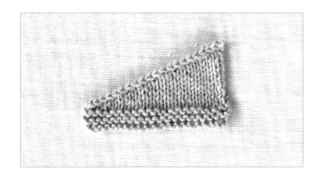

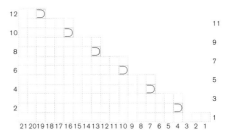

LEFT SIDE SLOPED TRIANGLE CHART

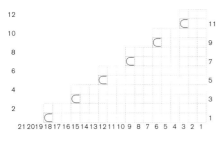

RIGHT SIDE SLOPED TRIANGLE CHART

creating a short row wedge sloping on both sides

A short row wedge is created by working short rows at both ends of your work. It is essentially each of our previous sloped swatches worked together (so you never reach the end of either a right-side or a wrong-side row).

The first example is similar to the short rows we worked in our short row basic swatches. The short rows are worked from the widest point to the narrowest point.

This can also be reversed to create a different effect by starting with the narrowest point and then working the short rows farther out with each row.

changing the curve

Now that you have the basics of short row shaping, you can create more complex shapes by varying the number of stitches between each short row. When short rows have more stitches between them, they create a shallower slope. When they are closer together (fewer stitches), the slope is much steeper.

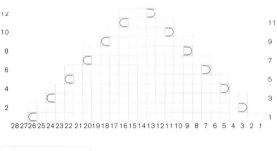

DOUBLE SLOPE CHART

Key

K on RS, p on WS

Short row turn

Short row turn

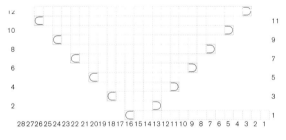

DOUBLE SLOPE CHART

Key

K on RS, p on WS

Short row turn

Short row turn

I've charted this out to show how the size of the short row steps influences the slope.

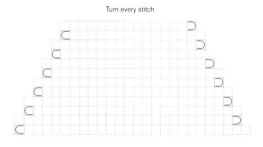

Turn every stitch

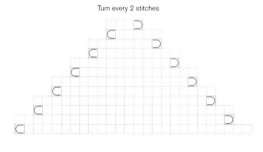

Turn every 2 stitches

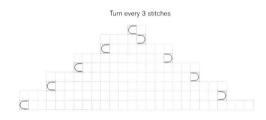

Turn every 3 stitches

Key

K on RS, p on WS

Short row turn

Short row turn

Creating 2-D Shawl Shapes with Short Rows

Short rows are an amazing way to create curves in a shawl. You have complete control over how the finished shape will look, and it can all be done without even changing your stitch count.

Begin by swatching different shapes with short rows, using the technique that you like best. Label them carefully and keep them as reference for your future short row projects. Using the techniques in this section, you can modify the shape of a short row shawl very easily. Just graph the shape you want on paper and then use that as a guide for working your short rows.

Here are my steps to shape a shawl curve organically. First, I use knitting graph paper to chart out the shape of my shawl, drawing the curve that I want to achieve. From there, I can decide on the spacing for the short rows, drawing them in as a series of steps.

Note: The boxes on knitting graph paper imitate the shape of the knitted stitch, so each unit is wider than it is tall—similar to a stitch. If you do an Internet search for "knitting graph paper," you can find examples to download.

You can see in the sketch on page 47 that changing from wide steps to narrow ones creates a bell-shaped curve that progresses from shallow to steep. I have created a curve on both ends that moves from three stitches between each turn, to two, and then finally to one. This creates a smooth bell curve.

The next step is to convert the sketch into more formal directions. I have shown it in chart form, but this can also be created as written directions.

Finally, I've swatched the chart in garter stitch. Garter stitch is ideal for creating short row curved shawls, as it is much more vertically compressed than stockinette stitch. This makes it easier to create a smooth curve, without creating too deep a shawl. The stitch-to-row ratio for stockinette is usually 2:3 or 3:4, but it is almost 1:2 for garter stitch.

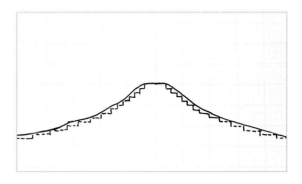

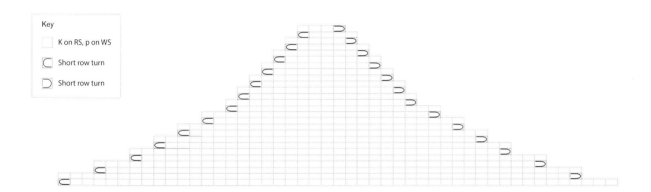

Key

☐ K on RS, p on WS

☐ Short row turn

☐ Short row turn

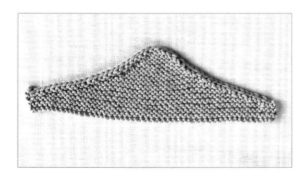

Creating 3-D Curves with Short Rows

We can also create three-dimensional shapes using short rows. When we work each row for a different length, it naturally begins to curve the fabric. When a series of short row wedges are built one on top of the other, they begin to create a curve in that direction. This is ideal for creating hoods, caps, and even balls.

When a short row wedge is created moving first inward and then out again, you create a right-angle corner that changes the direction of the work. One of the most useful applications is in creating the heel of a sock.

shaping hats

Using short rows that are worked on one side only, you can create a curve in your fabric. This is the basic idea used to knit a hat from side to side. When you begin working a hat from the side, you want the brim (at one end) to be the widest and the top of the crown the narrowest, which forms a wedge shape. With this repeatable wedge pattern, you can build the hat from side to side until you have the size you want.

In the diagram below, you can see the wedges of the hat shown flat. Each separate wedge is wider at the outer edge (brim) and narrower on the inside (crown

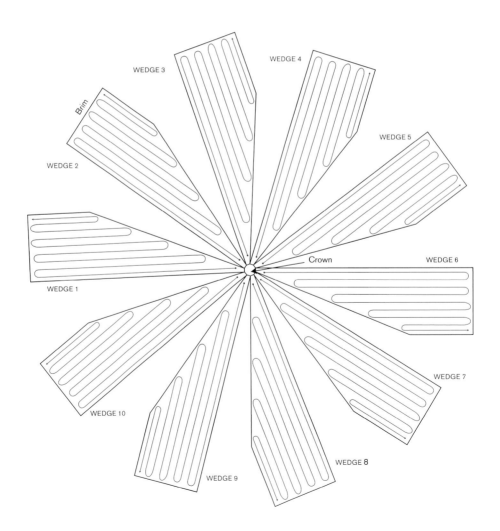

WEDGE 3

WEDGE 4

Brim

WEDGE 2

WEDGE 5

WEDGE 1

Crown

WEDGE 6

WEDGE 7

WEDGE 10

WEDGE 8

WEDGE 9

of hat). Even though the wedge shapes don't look like they should fit together, the short rows force them into the shape of the hat by curving the work. This creates a smaller size at the crown and a wider size at the brim.

shaping sock heels

Using short rows to change the direction of the knitted work creates the heels of socks. When you knit a sock from the cuff, you begin with a tube for the leg worked vertically down. Then to turn the corner at the heel, rotate your work so that you are now working horizontally to the toe.

To do this with short rows, you work a short row wedge across the heel stitches, working from the widest point to the narrowest (about one-third of the heel). When turns are worked, one fewer stitch is worked on each short row at each side so that the slope is very steep. Once you reach the narrowest point, you want to complete the right-angle turn, so you begin working a second short row wedge on top of the first one. However, this time you are working from the narrowest point back out to the widest point. This double set of short rows means that as you are increasing back out, you are working a double set of short rows (two wraps or yarn overs are worked together with the stitch every time). The techniques used are the very same as for the basic short rows, except you will be picking up two wraps instead of one every time you pass a set of previous short rows.

In the chart at right, you can see that there are fewer rows worked at each outer end between the red and blue lines. Even though these lines are far apart in the chart, they will be touching each other when you are knitting. This is what forces the heel to change direction, effectively using those short rows to pull your knitting in the direction you want it to go.

This technique is also used to create a short row toe, curving from the bottom of the foot to the top with short rows shaping the toe.

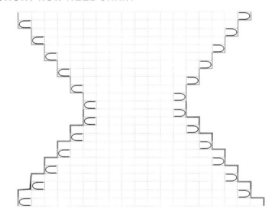

SHORT ROW HEEL CHART

Key

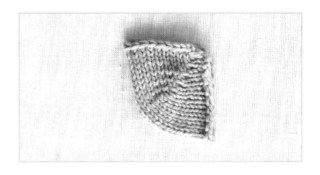

	K on RS, p on WS
	Short row turn
	Short row turn

tempisque
STRIPED GARTER STITCH SHAWL

This shawl uses short rows to form wedges in different colors that create a unique geometric shawl. Worked from the top down, increases at each end grow the shawl as you knit. The short rows do all the work in this shawl, creating complex shapes, yet you never use more than one color at a time. Even a newer knitter can tackle this pattern, thanks to basic stitches and German short rows.

Skill Level Beginner

Size One size

Finished Measurements
Width: 56" (142cm)
Depth: 14" (35.5cm)

Materials

YARN
Berroco Ultra Alpaca Light, 50% alpaca, 50% wool, 1.75 oz (50g), 144 yd (133m), 1 skein in 4266 (C1), 1 skein in 4279 (C2), 2 skeins in 42104 (C3) **2** fine

NEEDLES & NOTIONS
1 US size 8 (5mm) circular needle, 40" (101.5cm) long
Adjust needle size as necessary to achieve gauge.
US size H-8 (5mm) crochet hook for provisional cast-on
Waste yarn for provisional cast-on
Stitch markers
Tapestry needle

Gauge
16 stitches and 25 rows = 4" (10cm) in stockinette stitch, blocked
16 stitches and 32 rows = 4" (10cm) in garter stitch, blocked

Short Row Method Used
German (page 18)

Techniques
For other techniques used in the pattern, please refer to General Techniques (page 155).

Pattern Notes
- Slip the first stitch along the edge purlwise with the yarn in front. This creates a smooth edge on the shawl.
- When you are changing color, slip the first stitch purlwise with the yarn in front using the color from the previous row, then bring the yarn to the back and pick up the new color from behind.
- When counting stitches, take care to count each double stitch from the German short rows as only one stitch.

SHAWL BODY

Using C1, cast on 3 stitches with provisional cast-on method.

Knit 6 rows (3 garter ridge bumps). At end of the final row, do not turn; place marker, pick up 3 stitches from the edge of the work (3 bumps), place marker, undo provisional cast-on, and place the 3 stitches on the needle, k3—9 stitches.

Next row (WS): K3, slip marker, p3, slip marker, k3.

Inc Row 1 (RS): K3, slip marker, yo, kfb, yo, kfb, yo, kfb, yo, slip marker, k3—16 stitches.

Next row (WS): K3, slip marker, purl to marker, slip marker, k3.

Next row (RS): K3, slip marker, knit to marker, slip marker, k3.

Work 3 more rows in pattern established.

Inc Row 2 (RS): K3, slip marker, *k1, yo; repeat from * 9 more times, slip marker, k3—26 stitches.

Next row (WS): K3, slip marker, purl to marker, slip marker, k3.

Next row (RS): K3, slip marker, knit to marker, slip marker, k3.

Work 5 more rows in pattern established.

Inc Row 3 (RS): K3, slip marker, *k1, yo; repeat from * 19 more times, slip marker, k3—46 stitches.

Next row (WS): K3, slip marker, purl to marker, slip marker, k3.

Next row (RS): K3, slip marker, knit to marker, slip marker, k3.

Work 1 more wrong-side row.

Short Row 1 (RS): Using C2, k3, slip marker, yo, work to last 3 stitches, turn—1 stitch increased.

Short Row 2 (WS): With yarn in front, slip next stitch, pull yarn over needle to create double stitch, knit to marker, yo, slip marker, k3—1 stitch increased.

Short Row 3 (RS): Using C1, k3, slip marker, yo, knit to 2 stitches before the previous double stitch, turn—1 stitch increased.

Short Row 4 (WS): With yarn in front, slip next stitch, pull yarn over needle to create double stitch, knit to marker, yo, slip marker, k3—1 stitch increased.

Short Row 5 (RS): Using C2, k3, slip marker, yo, knit to 2 stitches before the previous double stitch, turn—1 stitch increased.

Short Row 6 (WS): With yarn in front, slip next stitch, pull yarn over needle to create double stitch, knit to marker, yo, slip marker, k3—1 stitch increased.

Repeat short rows 3–6 eight more times—84 stitches.

Break C1.

Short Row 7 (RS): Using C3, k3, slip marker, yo, k58, turn—1 stitch increased.

Short Row 8 (WS): With yarn in front, slip next stitch, pull yarn over needle to create double stitch, knit to marker, yo, slip marker, k3—1 stitch increased.

Short Row 9 (RS): Using C2, k3, slip marker, yo, knit to 2 stitches before the previous double stitch, turn—1 stitch increased.

Short Row 10 (WS): With yarn in front, slip next stitch, pull yarn over needle to create double stitch, knit to marker, yo, slip marker, k3—1 stitch increased.

Short Row 11 (RS): Using C3, k3, slip marker, yo, knit to 2 stitches before the previous double stitch, turn—1 stitch increased.

Short Row 12 (WS): With yarn in front, slip next stitch, pull yarn over needle to create double stitch, knit to marker, yo, slip marker, k3—1 stitch increased.

Repeat short rows 9–12 seven more times, then work short rows 9 and 10 once more—120 stitches.

Next row (RS): Using C3, k3, slip marker, yo, knit to last 3 stitches, yo, k3—122 stitches.

Short Row 13 (WS): K3, slip marker, yo, p77, turn work—1 stitch increased.

Short Row 14 (RS): With yarn in front, slip next stitch, pull yarn over needle to create double stitch, knit to marker, yo, slip marker, k3—1 stitch increased.

Short Row 15 (WS): K3, slip marker, yo, purl to 2 stitches before the previous double stitch, turn—1 stitch increased.

Short Row 16 (RS): With yarn in front, slip next stitch, pull yarn over needle to create double stitch, knit to marker, yo, slip marker, k3—1 stitch increased.

Repeat short rows 15 and 16 twenty-eight more times—182 stitches.

Next row (WS): K3, slip marker, yo, knit to marker, yo, slip marker, k3—2 stitches increased.

Edging Rows 1 and 2: Using C2, k3, yo, knit to last 3 stitches, yo, k3—2 stitches increased.

Edging Rows 3 and 4: Using C3, k3, yo, knit to last 3 stitches, yo, k3—2 stitches increased.

Repeat edging rows 1–4 five more times—232 stitches.

Edging Rows 5 and 6: Using C1, k3, yo, knit to last 3 stitches, yo, k3—2 stitches increased.

Edging Rows 7 and 8: Using C3, k3, yo, knit to last 3 stitches, yo, k3—2 stitches increased.

Repeat edging rows 5–8 five more times—280 stitches.

Using C1, knit 1 row. Bind off all stitches using elastic bind-off.

FINISHING
Weave in all ends. Block to correct dimensions.

celeste

CURVED LACE WRAP

Begin this wrap by casting on the full width of the wrap and then use short rows to create its curved shape. A delicate lace edging adds the perfect finishing touch. A heavier DK-weight yarn with a lovely halo is used with larger needles so that the lace is very open and drapey.

Skill Level Intermediate

Size One size

Finished Measurements
Width: 67" (170cm)
Depth: 20" (51cm)

Materials

YARN

2 skeins Bare Naked Wools Stone Soup DK, 80% wool, 15% alpaca, 5% Tencel/bamboo/silk/bison, 4 oz (115g), 300 yd (274m), in Granite ⓛ light

NEEDLES & NOTIONS

1 US size 8 (5mm) circular needle, 47" (119.5cm) long
Adjust needle size as necessary to achieve gauge.
Lockable stitch markers
Safety pins for Japanese short rows
Tapestry needle

Gauge

16 stitches and 25 rows = 4" (10cm) in stockinette stitch, blocked
Lace chart measures 5¾" (14.5cm) wide and 5" (12.5cm) deep

Short Row Method Used
Japanese (page 14)

Techniques

For other techniques used in the pattern, please refer to General Techniques (page 155).

PICOT CAST-ON

*Cast on 6 stitches using cable cast-on, bind off 2 stitches, slip stitch from right needle to left needle; repeat from * until desired number of stitches have been cast on.

LACE CHART (19-STITCH REPEAT)

Rows 1, 3, 5, and 7 (RS): Ssk, k3, (yo, ssk) twice, yo, k1, (yo, k2tog) twice, yo, k3, k2tog.
All WS rows: Purl.
Row 9 (RS): Ssk, k2, (yo, k2tog) twice, yo, k3, (yo, ssk) twice, yo, k2, k2tog.

Row 11 (RS): Ssk, k1, (yo, k2tog) twice, yo, k5, (yo, ssk) twice, yo, k1, k2tog.

Row 13 (RS): Ssk, (yo, k2tog) twice, yo, k7, (yo, ssk) twice, yo, k2tog.

Row 15 (RS): (yo, k2tog) twice, yo, k3, k2tog, k4, (yo, ssk) twice, yo, k2tog.

Rows 17 and 19 (RS): k1, (yo, k2tog) twice, yo, k3, k2tog, ssk, k3, (yo, ssk) twice, yo.

Row 21 (RS): k2, (yo, k2tog) twice, yo, k2, k2tog, ssk, k2, (yo, ssk) twice, yo, k1.

Row 23 (RS): k3, (yo, k2tog) twice, yo, k1, k2tog, ssk, k1, (yo, ssk) twice, yo, k2.

Row 25 (RS): k4, (yo, k2tog) 3 times, (ssk, yo) 3 times, k3.

Row 27 (RS): k6, yo, (k2tog, yo, ssk) twice, yo, k5.

Pattern Notes

When you are working many short rows from the widest point to the narrowest, it is helpful to place a lockable marker at the gap and move it every row for easier tracking.

WRAP BODY

Cast on 268 stitches using picot cast-on.

Work 6 rows in garter stitch.

Short Row 1 (RS): Knit to last 4 stitches, turn work.

Short Row 2 (WS): Slip stitch, place safety pin, purl to last 4 stitches, turn work.

Short Row 3 (RS): Slip stitch, place safety pin, knit to 4 stitches before previous gap, turn work.

Short Row 4 (WS): Slip stitch, place safety pin, purl to 4 stitches before previous gap, turn work.

Work short rows 3 and 4 seven more times.

Short Row 5 (RS): Slip stitch, place safety pin, knit to 3 stitches before previous gap, turn work.

Short Row 6 (WS): Slip stitch, place safety pin, purl to 3 stitches before previous gap, turn work.

Work short rows 5 and 6 eleven more times.

Short Row 7 (RS): Slip stitch, place safety pin, knit to 2 stitches before previous gap, turn work.

Short Row 8 (WS): Slip stitch, place safety pin, purl to 2 stitches before previous gap, turn work.

Work short rows 7 and 8 fourteen more times.

Short Row 9 (RS): Slip stitch, place safety pin, knit to 1 stitch before previous gap, turn work.

LACE CHART

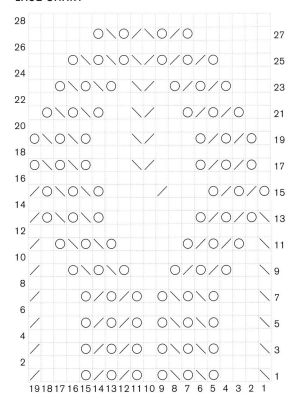

Short Row 10 (WS): Slip stitch, place safety pin, purl to 1 stitch before previous gap, turn work.

Work short rows 9 and 10 seven more times.

Next row (RS): Slip stitch, place safety pin, knit to end of row, working each yarn loop with the corresponding stitch.

Next row (WS): Purl to end of row, working each yarn loop with the corresponding stitch.

EDGING

Next row (RS): K1, work lace chart 14 times, k1.

Next row (WS): P1, work lace chart 14 times, p1.

Work these 2 rows 13 more times until lace chart is complete.

Bind off all stitches using elastic bind-off.

FINISHING

Weave in all ends. Block to correct dimensions.

diamante
CENTER-OUT SHAWL

This shawl has a unique architecture that forms short row "wings," which curve naturally over the shoulder. The shawl is worked from the center out with a spiraling lace repeat that is quick to memorize. From there, short row garter-stitch wings are worked at each side. The high silk content of the yarn allows the shawl to drape beautifully.

Skill Level Intermediate

Size One size

Finished Measurements
Width: 52" (132cm)
Depth: 35½" (90cm)

Materials

YARN

2 skeins Blue Moon Fiber Arts Marine Silk Fingering, 51% silk, 29% merino, 20% SeaCell rayon, 3.5 oz (100g), 487 yd (445m), in Irish Girlie Green  super fine

NEEDLES & NOTIONS
Set of US size 7 (4.5mm) double-pointed needles
1 US size 7 (4.5mm) circular needle, 32" (81cm) long
Adjust needle size as necessary to achieve gauge.
Waste yarn
Stitch markers
Spare needle
Tapestry needle

Gauge
16 stitches and 22 rows = 4" (10cm) in spiral lace pattern, blocked
16 stitches and 24 rows = 4" (10cm) in garter stitch, blocked

Short Row Method Used
German (page 18)

Techniques
For other techniques used in the pattern, please refer to General Techniques (page 155).

4-STITCH I-CORD

With double-pointed needles, cast on 4 stitches, *k4, slip 4 stitches just worked to the other end of the double-pointed needle and tug yarn snugly; repeat from * until I-cord is desired length.

SPIRAL LACE CHART

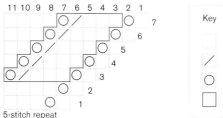 

5-stitch repeat

Note: Full written directions for the chart are given in the pattern.

Pattern Notes

- It is important to remember that the German short rows used in this project create a double stitch. Do *not* include this extra stitch in your stitch counts.
- This shawl is worked from the center of the back outward. Each wing is shaped separately using short rows.

SHAWL CENTER

With double-pointed needles and waste yarn, work 4-stitch I-cord for approximately 1" (2.5cm).

Drop waste yarn and begin knitting in the round with working yarn, redistributing stitches evenly across double-pointed needles when possible.

Inc Rnd 1: (Kfb) 4 times—8 stitches.

Inc Rnd 2: (Kfb) 8 times—16 stitches.

We are now working from the spiral lace chart; use chart or written directions below. Switch from double-pointed to circular needles when there are sufficient stitches.

Rnd 1: *K1, yo, k3, place marker; repeat from * 3 more times (with final marker being start of round)—20 stitches.

Rnd 2: *K1, yo, k4; repeat from * 3 more times—24 stitches.

Rnd 3: *K1, yo, (k3, k2tog, yo) repeat to marker; repeat from * 3 more times—4 stitches increased.

Rnd 4: *K1, yo, (k3, k2tog, yo) repeat to last stitch before marker, k1; repeat from * 3 more times.

Rnd 5: *K1, yo, (k3, k2tog, yo) repeat to last 2 stitches before marker, k2; repeat from * 3 more times.

Rnd 6: *K1, yo, (k3, k2tog, yo) repeat to last 3 stitches before marker, k3; repeat from * 3 more times.

Rnd 7: *K1, yo, (k3, k2tog, yo) repeat to last 4 stitches before marker, k4; repeat from * 3 more times.

Work rnds 3–7 sixteen more times—364 stitches.

Edging Rnd 1: *P1, yo, purl to marker, slip marker; repeat from * 3 more times—368 stitches.

Edging Rnd 2: *K1, yo, knit to marker; repeat from * 3 more times—372 stitches.

Repeat these 2 rounds 3 more times. Work edging rnd 1 once more—400 stitches.

Bind-Off Rnd: Bind off 200 stitches using elastic bind-off, knit to end of round. Slip first set of 100 stitches to spare needle to be held for later.

At this point you can split the remaining yarn into 2 skeins to ensure you have enough for both sides; alternatively, weigh yarn as you work.

LEFT WING
Wedge 1
With second set of 100 stitches on needles, turn so wrong side is facing for next row.

Next row (WS): Slip 1 purlwise with yarn in front, knit to last stitch, turn work.

Next row (RS) and all following RS rows: Slip 1 purlwise with yarn in front, pulling yarn over needle so that 2 strands are visible at top of needle, knit to end of row.

Next row (WS): Slip 1 purlwise with yarn in front, knit to 5 stitches before double stitch, turn work.

Next row (RS): Work as for previous right-side row.

***Next row (WS):** Slip 1 purlwise with yarn in front, knit to 6 stitches before double stitch, turn work.

Next row (RS): Work as for previous right-side row.

Repeat last 2 rows 11 more times.*

Wedge 2

Next row (WS): Slip 1 purlwise with yarn in front, knit to last 2 stitches (*working every double stitch as k2tog*), turn work.

Next row (RS) and all following RS rows: Slip 1 purlwise with yarn in front, pulling yarn over needle so that 2 strands are visible at top of needle, knit to end of row.

Next row (WS): Slip 1 purlwise with yarn in front, knit to 4 stitches before double stitch, turn work.

Next row (RS): Work as for previous right-side row.

Repeat from * to * as in Wedge 1.

Wedge 3

Next row (WS): Slip 1 purlwise with yarn in front, knit to last 3 stitches (*working every double stitch as k2tog*), turn work.

Next row (RS) and all following RS rows: Slip 1 purlwise with yarn in front, pulling yarn over needle so that 2 strands are visible at top of needle, knit to end of row.

Next row (WS): Slip 1 purlwise with yarn in front, knit to 3 stitches before double stitch, turn work.

Next row (RS): Work as for previous right-side row.

Repeat from * to * as in Wedge 1.

Wedge 4

Next row (WS): Slip 1 purlwise with yarn in front, knit to last 4 stitches (*working every double stitch as k2tog*), turn work.

Next row (RS) and all following RS rows: Slip 1 purlwise with yarn in front, pulling yarn over needle so that 2 strands are visible at top of needle, knit to end of row.

Next row (WS): Slip 1 purlwise with yarn in front, knit to 2 stitches before double stitch, turn work.

Next row (RS): Work as for previous right-side row.

Repeat from * to * as in Wedge 1.

Wedge 5

Next row (WS): Slip 1 purlwise with yarn in front, knit to last 5 stitches (*working every double stitch as k2tog*), turn work.

Next row (RS) and all following RS rows: Slip 1 purlwise with yarn in front, pulling yarn over needle so that 2 strands are visible at top of needle, knit to end of row.

Next row (WS): Slip 1 purlwise with yarn in front, knit to 1 stitch before double stitch, turn work.

Next row (RS): Work as for previous right-side row.

Repeat from * to * as in Wedge 1.

Wedge 6

Next row (WS): Slip 1 purlwise with yarn in front, knit to last 6 stitches (*working every double stitch as k2tog*), turn work.

Next row (RS) and all following RS rows: Slip 1 purlwise with yarn in front, pulling yarn over needle so that 2 strands are visible at top of needle, knit to end of row.

Next row (WS): Slip 1 purlwise with yarn in front, knit to double stitch, turn work.

Next row (RS): Work as for previous right-side row.

Repeat from * to * as in Wedge 1.

Next row (WS): Slip 1 purlwise with yarn in front, knit all stitches (*working every double stitch as k2tog*).

Next row (RS): Slip 1 purlwise with yarn in front, knit to end of row.

Bind-Off Row (WS): Bind off all stitches using elastic bind-off.

Note: If you run out of half your yarn before finishing Wedge 6, omit the final few short rows and ensure that you do the same for the Right Wing.

RIGHT WING

Starting on a wrong-side row, join yarn to remaining 100 stitches on right wing.

Wedge 1

Next row (WS): Knit to end of row.

Next row (RS): Slip 1 purlwise with yarn in front, knit to last stitch, turn work.

Next row (WS) and all following WS rows: Slip 1 purlwise with yarn in front, pulling yarn over needle so that 2 strands are visible at top of needle, knit to end of row.

Next row (RS): Slip 1 purlwise with yarn in front, knit to 5 stitches before double stitch, turn work.

*****Next row (WS):** Work as for previous wrong-side row.

Next row (RS): Slip 1 purlwise with yarn in front, knit to 6 stitches before double stitch, turn work.

Repeat last 2 rows 11 more times.*

Wedge 2

Next row (WS): Work as for previous wrong-side row.

Next row (RS): Slip 1 purlwise with yarn in front, knit to last 2 stitches (*working every double stitch as k2tog*), turn work.

Next row (WS): Work as for previous wrong-side row.

Next row (RS): Slip 1 purlwise with yarn in front, knit to 4 stitches before double stitch, turn work.

Repeat from * to * as in Wedge 1.

Wedge 3

Next row (WS): Work as for previous wrong-side row.

Next row (RS): Slip 1 purlwise with yarn in front, knit to last 3 stitches (*working every double stitch as k2tog*), turn work.

Next row (WS): Work as for previous wrong-side row.

Next row (RS): Slip 1 purlwise with yarn in front, knit to 3 stitches before double stitch, turn work.

Repeat from * to * as in Wedge 1.

Wedge 4

Next row (WS): Work as for previous wrong-side row.

Next row (RS): Slip 1 purlwise with yarn in front, knit to last 4 stitches (*working every double stitch as k2tog*), turn work.

Next row (WS): Work as for previous wrong-side row.

Next row (RS): Slip 1 purlwise with yarn in front, knit to 2 stitches before double stitch, turn work.

Repeat from * to * as in Wedge 1.

Wedge 5

Next row (WS): Work as for previous wrong-side row.

Next row (RS): Slip 1 purlwise with yarn in front, knit to last 5 stitches (*working every double stitch as k2tog*), turn work.

Next row (WS): Work as for previous wrong-side row.

Next row (RS): Slip 1 purlwise with yarn in front, knit to 1 stitch before double stitch, turn work.

Repeat from * to * as in Wedge 1.

Wedge 6

Next row (WS): Work as for previous wrong-side row.

Next row (RS): Slip 1 purlwise with yarn in front, knit to last 6 stitches (*working every double stitch as k2tog*), turn work.

Next row (WS): Work as for previous wrong-side row.

Next row (RS): Slip 1 purlwise with yarn in front, knit to double stitch, turn work.

Repeat from * to * as in Wedge 1.

Next row (WS): Work as for previous wrong-side row.

Next row (RS): Slip 1 purlwise with yarn in front, knit to end of row (*working every double stitch as k2tog*).

Bind-Off Row (WS): Bind off all stitches using elastic bind-off.

FINISHING

Carefully remove waste-yarn I-cord from center and place these 4 working yarn stitches on needle. With a tapestry needle, thread yarn tail through these stitches, tighten, and fasten off.

Weave in all ends. Block to correct dimensions. Note that this shawl is blocked aggressively to open up the lace.

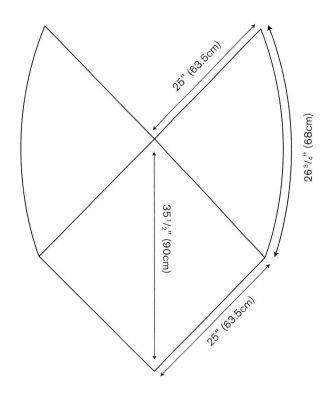

MODULAR WEDGE SCARF

This wrap is worked as a series of wedges, alternating a highly variegated yarn with a complementary solid color. Each wedge is shaped differently, making it a great project to practice short rows in garter stitch. Wrapped in layers like a shawl or worn long like a scarf, it gives you a huge variety of styling options.

Skill Level Intermediate

Size One size

Finished Measurements
Width: 80" (203cm)
Depth: 10" (25.5cm) at center

Materials

YARN
Sweet Georgia Silk Crush, 50% superwash merino, 50% silk, 4 oz (115g), 375 yd (343m), 1 skein in Phoenix Rising (C1), 1 skein in Cayenne (C2) **1** super fine

NEEDLES & NOTIONS
1 US size 7 (4.5mm) circular needle, 32" (81cm) long
Adjust needle size as necessary to achieve gauge.
Tapestry needle

Gauge
16 stitches and 26 rows = 4" (10cm) in stockinette stitch, blocked
16 stitches and 40 rows = 4" (10cm) in garter stitch, blocked

Short Row Method Used
Wrap and Turn (page 10)

Techniques
For other techniques used in the pattern, please refer to General Techniques (page 155).

APPLIED I-CORD
*K2, slip 1 knitwise, pick up and knit stitch from the edge of the work, pass slipped stitch over, slip all 3 stitches back to left needle; repeat from * until all stitches have been worked—3 I-cord stitches remain on needle. K3tog, break yarn, and draw yarn through final stitch.

CENTER TRIANGLE

With C1, cast on 1 stitch.

Next row (RS): Yo, knit all stitches—1 stitch increased.

Next row (WS): Yo, knit all stitches—1 stitch increased.

Repeat these 2 rows 49 more times—101 stitches.

Bind off all stitches using elastic bind-off.

RIGHT SIDE

Right Wedge 1

Using C2, with right side of work facing and starting at the bottom right of the Center Triangle, pick up and knit a stitch in every loop up to the top edge of the triangle—50 stitches.

Next row (WS): Cast on 20 stitches using cable cast-on, knit to end of row—70 stitches.

Next row (RS): Knit to end of row.

Next row (WS): Knit to last 2 stitches, w&t.

Next row (RS): Knit to end of row.

Next row (WS): Knit to 2 stitches before previously wrapped stitch, w&t.

Next row (RS): Knit to end of row.

Next row (WS): Purl to 2 stitches before previously wrapped stitch, w&t.

Next row (RS): Knit to end of row.

Repeat these last 2 rows 30 more times.

Next row (WS): Purl, picking up and working wraps with the stitches they wrap as you pass them.

Work 6 rows in garter stitch.

Bind off all stitches using elastic bind-off.

Right Wedge 2

Using C1, cast on 30 stitches using long tail cast-on, then pick up and knit 35 stitches from right side of Right Wedge 1, starting at the bottom—65 stitches.

Note: Picked-up stitches do not extend all the way to the edge of Right Wedge 1; you will be picking up 2 stitches for every 3 rows.

Next row (WS): Knit.

*__Row 1 (RS):__ K1, M1R, knit to end of row.

Row 2 (WS): Knit.

Repeat these last 2 rows 4 more times—70 stitches.

SHORT ROW TRIANGLE

Short Row 1 (RS): K2, w&t.

Next row (WS): Purl all stitches.

Short Row 2 (RS): Knit to previously wrapped stitch, work wrap with stitch it wraps, k1, w&t.

Next row (WS): Purl all stitches.

Work these last 2 rows 9 more times.

Short Row 3 (RS): Knit to 2 stitches before previously wrapped stitch, w&t.

Next row (WS): Purl all stitches.

Work these last 2 rows 9 more times.

Next row (RS): Knit all stitches, working all wraps with stitches they wrap.

Next row (WS): Knit all stitches.*

Work from * to * twice more—80 stitches.

Row 1 (RS): K1, M1R, knit to end of row.

Row 2 (WS): Knit.

Repeat these 2 rows 4 more times—85 stitches.

Work row 1 once more—86 stitches.

Right Wedge 3

Row 1 (WS): Using C1, bind off 16 stitches, purl to end of row—70 stitches.

SECTION 1

Next row (RS): Using C2, knit to last stitch, w&t.

Next row (WS): Purl all stitches.

Next row (RS): Knit to 4 stitches before wrapped stitch, w&t.

Next row (WS): Purl all stitches.

*****Next row (RS):** Knit to 5 stitches before wrapped stitch, w&t.

Next row (WS): Purl all stitches.

Repeat last 2 rows 11 more times.*

SECTION 2

Next row (RS): Knit to last 2 stitches (*working every wrap you pass with the stitch it wraps*), w&t.

Next row (WS): Purl all stitches.

Next row (RS): Knit to 3 stitches before previously wrapped stitch, w&t.

Next row (WS): Purl all stitches.

Repeat from * to * as in Section 1.

SECTION 3

Next row (RS): Knit to last 3 stitches (*working every wrap you pass with the stitch it wraps*), w&t.

Next row (WS): Purl all stitches.

Next row (RS): Knit to 2 stitches before previously wrapped stitch, w&t.

Next row (WS): Purl all stitches.

Repeat from * to * from Section 1.

SECTION 4

Next row (RS): Knit to last 4 stitches (*working every wrap you pass with the stitch it wraps*), w&t.

Next row (WS): Purl all stitches.

Next row (RS): Knit to 1 stitch before previously wrapped stitch, w&t.

Next row (WS): Purl all stitches.

Repeat from * to * from Section 1.

Work all stitches in garter stitch for 6 rows, working all wraps with the stitch they wrap as you pass them. Break yarn.

Using C1, starting at the right edge of Right Wedge 3, work applied I-cord across the bottom until you reach the held stitches; turn corner and work I-cord bind-off across all 70 stitches.

LEFT SIDE

Left Wedge 1

Using C2, cast on 20 stitches using cable cast-on, knit all cast-on stitches, then with right side of work facing and starting at the top left of the Center Triangle, pick up and knit a stitch in every loop down to the bottom edge of the triangle—70 stitches.

Next row (WS): Knit to end of row.

Next row (RS): Knit to last 2 stitches, w&t.

Next row (WS): Knit to end of row.

Next row (RS): Knit to 2 stitches before previously wrapped stitch, w&t.

Next row (WS): Knit to end of row.

Next row (RS): Knit to 2 stitches before previously wrapped stitch, w&t.

Next row (WS): Purl to end of row.

Repeat these last 2 rows 30 more times.

Next row (RS): Knit to end of row, picking up and working wraps with the stitches they wrap as you pass them.

Next row (WS): Purl.

Work 6 rows in garter stitch.

Bind off all stitches using elastic bind-off.

Left Wedge 2

Using C1 on the left side of Left Wedge 1 and starting 24 rows down from top, pick up and knit 35 stitches.

Note: You will be picking up 2 stitches for every 3 rows.

Next row (WS): Cast on 30 stitches using cable cast-on method, knit to end of row—65 stitches.

*Row 1 (RS): Knit to last stitch, M1L, k1.

Row 2 (WS): Knit.

Repeat these 2 rows 3 more times. Work row 1 once more—70 stitches.

SHORT-ROW TRIANGLE

Short Row 1 (WS): P2, w&t.

Next row (RS): Knit all stitches.

Short Row 2 (WS): Purl to previously wrapped stitch, work wrap with stitch it wraps, p1, w&t.

Next row (RS): Knit all stitches.

Work these last 2 rows 9 more times.

Short Row 3 (WS): Purl to 2 stitches before previously wrapped stitch, w&t.

Next row (RS): Knit all stitches.

Work these last 2 rows 9 more times.

Next row (WS): Knit all stitches, working all wraps with stitches they wrap.

Next row (RS): Knit all stitches.*

Work from * to * twice more—80 stitches.

Row 1 (WS): Knit.

Row 2 (RS): Knit to last st, M1L, k1.

Repeat these 2 rows 5 more times—86 stitches. Work row 1 once more.

Left Wedge 3

Row 1 (RS): Using C1, bind off 16 stitches, knit to the end of the row—70 stitches.

SECTION 1

Next row (WS): Using C2, purl to last stitch, w&t.

Next row (RS): Knit all stitches.

Next row (WS): Purl to 4 stitches before wrapped stitch, w&t.

Next row (RS): Knit all stitches.

*__Next row (WS):__ Purl to 5 stitches before wrapped stitch, w&t.

Next row (RS): Knit all stitches.

Repeat last 2 rows 11 more times.*

SECTION 2

Next row (WS): Purl to last 2 stitches (*working every wrap you pass with the stitch it wraps*), w&t.

Next row (RS): Knit all stitches.

Next row (WS): Purl to 3 stitches before previously wrapped stitch, w&t.

Next row (RS): Knit all stitches.

Repeat from * to * from Section 1.

SECTION 3

Next row (WS): Purl to last 3 stitches (*working every wrap you pass with the stitch it wraps*), w&t.

Next row (RS): Knit all stitches.

Next row (WS): Purl to 2 stitches before previously wrapped stitch, w&t.

Next row (RS): Knit all stitches.

Repeat from * to * from Section 1.

SECTION 4

Next row (WS): Purl to last 4 stitches (*working every wrap you pass with the stitch it wraps*), w&t.

Next row (RS): Knit all stitches.

Next row (WS): Purl to 1 stitch before previously wrapped stitch, w&t.

Next row (RS): Knit all stitches.

Repeat from * to * from Section 1.

Work all stitches in garter stitch for 5 rows, working all wraps with the stitch they wrap as you pass them. Work I-cord bind-off across all 70 stitches; turn corner and work applied I-cord across the bottom of Left Wedge 3.

FINISHING

Weave in all ends. Block to dimensions shown on schematic.

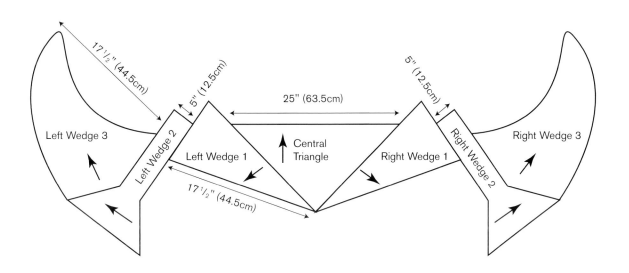

claro

BASIC TOP-DOWN SOCK

Two different yarns are shown in the samples: a rainbow, self-striping, single-ply yarn and a neutral high-twist yarn that makes a practical yet luxurious gift. The design sports a short row heel and toe, as well as a gusset at the instep; I find that socks with a gusset have a better fit. If you have a low instep, you can omit the gusset increases and decreases.

Skill Level Beginner

Sizes To fit foot circumference up to 8½ (9½, 10½)" (21.5 [24, 26.5]cm)

Finished Measurements
Actual sock circumference: 7½ (8½, 9½)" (19 [21.5, 24]cm)
Sizes 7½" (19cm) and 9½" (24cm) modeled with 1" (2.5cm) negative ease

Materials

YARN
Small sample (opposite): 1 (1, 1) skein Schoppel Wolle Zauberball, 75% wool, 25% nylon, 3.5 oz (100g), 459 yd (420m), in 1564  super fine
Large sample (see page 73): 1 (1, 1) skein Susquehanna Knitting Company Susquehanna Sock, 75% superwash merino, 25% nylon, 3.5 oz (100g), 463 yds (423m), in Spicy Brown  super fine

NEEDLES & NOTIONS
1 US size 1½ (2.5mm) circular needle, 40" (101.5cm) long, for Magic Loop
or
1 set US size 1½ (2.5mm) double-pointed needles
Adjust needle size as necessary to achieve gauge.
Tapestry needle

Gauge
32 stitches and 44 rows = 4" (10cm) in stockinette stitch

Short Row Method Used
Wrap and Turn (page 10)

Techniques
For other techniques used in the pattern, please refer to General Techniques (page 155).

Pattern Notes

- I describe the short rows for the heel and toe as wrap-and-turn short rows, but you can substitute your preferred short row method. To use the yarn-over method, see Arenal Cabled Toe-Up Sock (page 74) for details. If you use the Japanese method, I advise using waste yarn to hold the yarn loops (page 14), as there are many short rows. Work the turns as shown in the techniques section (page 14), but when you work the second layer of short rows, remember to pick up both the top and bottom loops every time you need to knit them with the stitch.
- I used the Magic Loop method for circular knitting, but double-pointed needles can be used if you prefer. With Magic Loop, half of the stitches are on each side of the cable, which means your heel stitches are on one side and your instep stitches are on the other.
- When casting on, some knitters hold two needles together to enlarge the cast-on stitches and ensure the cast-on edge is loose enough to stretch over the foot.

LEG

Cast on 60 (68, 76) stitches loosely and join to work in the round, taking care not to twist stitches.

Ribbing Rnd: *K1 tbl, p1; repeat from * to end of round.

Work 14 more ribbing rnds.

Work in stockinette stitch until leg measures 6½ (7, 7½)" (16.5 [18, 19]cm) from top of cuff, or desired length.

GUSSET INCREASES

The first 30 (34, 38) stitches on the needle will be the heel stitches, and the next 30 (34, 38) stitches will be the instep stitches. Gusset increases are worked at each end of the instep stitches.

Inc Rnd: K30 (34, 38) stitches, k1, M1L, knit to last instep stitch, M1R, k1—2 stitches increased.

Work inc rnd 8 (9, 10) more times—78 (88, 98) stitches.

SHORT ROW HEEL

48 (54, 60) instep stitches will remain unworked on one side of the Magic Loop while you work short rows back and forth on the heel stitches only.

Short Row 1 (RS): Knit to last heel stitch, w&t.

Short Row 2 (WS): Purl to last heel stitch, w&t.

Short Row 3 (RS): Knit to 1 stitch before previously wrapped stitch, w&t.

Short Row 4 (WS): Purl to 1 stitch before previously wrapped stitch, w&t.

Repeat short rows 3 and 4 as above 8 (9, 10) more times—10 (11, 12) stitches wrapped at each end, 10 (12, 14) stitches unwrapped at center.

Short Row 5 (RS): Knit to first wrapped stitch, knit wrap with stitch it wraps, w&t.

Note: This wrapped stitch will now have 2 wraps.

Short Row 6 (WS): Purl to first wrapped stitch, purl wrap with stitch it wraps, w&t.

Short Row 7 (RS): Knit to wrapped stitch, knit both wraps with stitch they wrap, w&t.

Short Row 8 (WS): Purl to wrapped stitch, purl both wraps with stitch they wrap, w&t.

Repeat short rows 7 and 8 as above 7 (8, 9) more times—1 wrapped stitch remains at each end.

Next rnd: Knit to last heel stitch, knit both wraps with stitch they wrap, knit instep stitches, knit both wraps with stitch they wrap (take care as wraps are on different sides), knit to end-of-heel stitches.

GUSSET DECREASE

Note: Start of round has now moved to start of instep stitches.

Dec Rnd: Ssk, knit to last 2 instep stitches, k2tog, knit all sole stitches—2 stitches decreased.

Next rnd: Knit.

Repeat these 2 rounds 8 (9, 10) more times—60 (68, 76) stitches.

FOOT

Work in stockinette stitch until foot measures 1¾ (2, 2¼)" (4.5 [5, 5.5]cm) less than desired total length.

Note: Suggested work length for average foot is 6¼ (7, 7¾)" (16 [18, 19.5]cm).

SHORT ROW TOE

Sole stitches will remain unworked on one side of the Magic Loop while you work short rows back and forth on the instep stitches only.

Short Row 1 (RS): Knit to last instep stitch, w&t.

Short Row 2 (WS): Purl to last instep stitch, w&t.

Short Row 3 (RS): Knit to 1 stitch before previously wrapped stitch, w&t.

Short Row 4 (WS): Purl to 1 stitch before previously wrapped stitch, w&t.

Repeat short rows 3 and 4 as above 8 (9, 10) more times—10 (11, 12) stitches wrapped at each end, 10 (12, 14) stitches unwrapped at center.

Short Row 5 (RS): Knit to first wrapped stitch, knit wrap with stitch it wraps, w&t.

Note: This wrapped stitch will now have 2 wraps.

Short Row 6 (WS): Purl to first wrapped stitch, purl wrap with stitch it wraps, w&t.

Short Row 7 (RS): Knit to wrapped stitch, knit both wraps with stitch they wrap, w&t.

Short Row 8 (WS): Purl to wrapped stitch, purl both wraps with stitch they wrap, w&t.

Repeat short rows 7 and 8 as above 7 (8, 9) more times—1 wrapped stitch remains at each end.

Next rnd: Knit to last instep stitch, knit both wraps with stitch they wrap.

With sole of sock facing, break yarn, leaving long tail.

Graft 30 (34, 38) stitches from sole with stitches from instep; the final instep stitch still has a wrap so this wrap will be worked together with the stitch when grafting.

FINISHING

Weave in all loose ends. Block sock to dimensions given.

arenal
CABLED TOE-UP SOCK

There are many different ways to knit a sock; in this pattern I'll give you the basics for creating a toe-up sock with a short row heel and toe. Using short rows, you can avoid the complex shaping usually needed for a sock heel. However, my added gussets create a much nicer fit than traditional short row heels.

Skill Level Intermediate

Sizes To fit foot circumference up to 8½ (9½, 10½)" (21.5 [24, 26.5]cm).

Finished Measurements
Actual sock circumference: 7½ (8½, 9½)" (19 [21.5, 24]cm)
Size 7½" (19cm) modeled with 1" (2.5cm) negative ease

Materials

YARN
1 (1, 1) skein Bare Naked Wools Breakfast Blend Fingering, 50% merino, 40% alpaca, 10% nylon, 4 oz (115g), 425 yd (389m), in Oatmeal  super fine

NEEDLES & NOTIONS
1 US size 1½ (2.5mm) circular needle, 40" (101.5cm) long, for Magic Loop
1 US size 0 (2mm) circular needle, 40" (101.5cm) long, for cuff
or
1 set US size 1½ (2.5mm) double-pointed needles

1 set US size 0 (2mm) double-pointed needles, for cuff
Adjust needle size as necessary to achieve gauge.
US size B-1 (2.25mm) crochet hook for provisional cast-on
Waste yarn for provisional cast-on
Stitch markers
Tapestry needle

Gauge
32 stitches and 44 rows = 4" (10cm) in stockinette stitch on larger needles, blocked
40 stitches and 44 rows = 4" (10cm) in pattern, on larger needles, blocked

Short Row Technique
Yarn Over (page 16)

Techniques
For other techniques used in the pattern, please refer to General Techniques (page 155).

Ltwist: Knit into back of second stitch on needle, leaving stitch on left-hand needle, knit into back of first stitch, slip both stitches off left-hand needle.

Rtwist: Knit into second stitch on needle, leaving stitch on left-hand needle, knit into first stitch, slip both stitches off left-hand needle.

RIGHT FOOT INSTEP PATTERN

Rnds 1, 2, and 3: *P2, k2; repeat from * to last 2 stitches, p2.
Rnd 4: *P2, Ltwist; repeat from * to last 2 stitches, p2.
Repeat rounds 1–4 for right foot instep pattern.

RIGHT LEG PATTERN

Rnds 1, 2, and 3: *K2, p2; repeat from * to end of round.
Rnd 4: *Ltwist, p2; repeat from * to end of round.
Repeat rounds 1–4 for right leg pattern.

LEFT FOOT INSTEP PATTERN

Rnds 1, 2, and 3: *P2, k2; repeat from * to last 2 stitches, p2.
Rnd 4: *P2, Rtwist; repeat from * to last 2 stitches, p2.
Repeat rounds 1–4 for left foot instep pattern.

LEFT LEG PATTERN

Rnds 1, 2, and 3: *K2, p2; repeat from * to end of round.
Rnd 4: *Rtwist, p2; repeat from * to end of round.
Repeat rounds 1–4 for left leg pattern.

Pattern Notes

- I've described the short rows for the heel and toe as yarn-over short rows. You can substitute your preferred short row method. With this method of short rows, when I refer to a "double stitch," I am talking about the yarn over and the stitch that is paired with it.
- I used the Magic Loop method for circular knitting but double-pointed needles can be used instead if you prefer. With Magic Loop, half of the stitches are on each side of the cable, which means the heel stitches are on one side and the instep stitches are on the other.

SHORT ROW TOE

Provisional cast-on stitches will remain unworked on waste yarn while you work short rows back and forth on the live stitches.

With larger-size needles, cast on 34 (38, 42) stitches using provisional cast-on and waste yarn.

Setup Row (WS): Purl 1 row with working yarn.

Short Row 1 (RS): K33 (37, 41), turn work.

Short Row 2 (WS): Yo, p32 (36, 40), turn work.

Short Row 3 (RS): Yo, knit to double stitch, turn work.

Short Row 4 (WS): Yo, purl to double stitch, turn work.

Repeat short rows 3 and 4 as above 9 (10, 11) more times.

Short Row 5 (RS): Yo, knit to first double stitch, knit stitch, k2tog (*yarn over and next stitch*), turn work.

Short Row 6 (WS): Yo (*there are now 2 yarn overs*), purl to first double stitch, purl stitch, ssp (*yarn over and next stitch*), turn work.

Short Row 7 (RS): Yo, knit to double stitch, knit stitch, k3tog (*both yarn overs and next stitch*), turn work.

Short Row 8 (WS): Yo, purl to double stitch, purl stitch, sssp (*both yarn overs and next stitch*), turn work.

Repeat short rows 7 and 8 as above 8 (9, 10) more times.

Next rnd: Yo, knit to last double stitch, knit stitch, k3tog, place marker for start of round, undo provisional cast-on, placing 34 (38, 42) stitches on left-hand needle, knit these 34 (38, 42) stitches, sssk (*final 2 yarn overs and stitch*), knit to end of round—68 (76, 84) stitches.

FOOT

Follow left and right foot instep pattern for foot being worked.

Next rnd: K34 (38, 42), work foot instep pattern to end.

Work in pattern as established until foot measures 4 (4¼, 4½)" (10 [11, 11.5]cm) less than desired total length.

Length to work for average foot is 4 (4¾, 5½)" (10 [12, 14]cm).

GUSSET INCREASES

The first 34 (38, 42) stitches on the needle are the heel stitches and the next 34 (38, 42) stitches are the instep stitches. Gusset increases are worked at either end of the instep stitches.

Inc Rnd: K34 (38, 42), M1L, work in pattern to the end of the round, M1R—2 stitches increased.

Next rnd: K34 (38, 42), knit gusset stitches, work appropriate foot instep pattern to gusset stitches, knit gusset stitches.

Work these 2 rounds 9 (10, 11) more times, working all gusset stitches in stockinette stitch—88 (98, 108) stitches; 34 (38, 42) heel stitches, 54 (60, 66) instep stitches with gusset.

SHORT ROW HEEL

While you work short rows back and forth on the heel stitches only, 54 (60, 66) instep stitches will remain unworked on one side of the Magic Loop.

Short Row 1 (RS): K33 (37, 41), turn work.

Short Row 2 (WS): Yo, p32 (36, 40), turn work.

Short Row 3 (RS): Yo, knit to double stitch, turn work.

Short Row 4 (WS): Yo, purl to double stitch, turn work.

Repeat short rows 3 and 4 as above 9 (10, 11) more times.

Short Row 5 (RS): Yo, knit to first double stitch, knit stitch, k2tog (*yarn over and next stitch*), turn work.

Short Row 6 (WS): Yo (*there are now 2 yarn overs*), purl to first double stitch, purl stitch, ssp (*yarn over and next stitch*), turn work.

Short Row 7 (RS): Yo, knit to double stitch, knit stitch, k3tog (*both yarn overs and next stitch*), turn work.

Short Row 8 (WS): Yo, purl to double stitch, purl stitch, sssp (*both yarn overs and next stitch*), turn work.

Repeat short rows 7 and 8 as above 8 (9, 10) more times.

Next rnd: Yo, knit to last double stitch, knit stitch, k3tog, work all instep stitches in appropriate foot instep pattern, remove marker for start of round, sssk (*final 2 yarn overs and stitch from start of next round*), place marker for new start of round.

Slip final heel stitch to instep stitches for gusset decreases—you will have 32 (36, 40) stitches on heel needle and 56 (62, 68) stitches on instep needle.

GUSSET DECREASE

Dec Rnd: Knit heel stitches, ssk, work in pattern to the last 2 instep stitches, k2tog—2 stitches decreased.

Repeat this round 9 (10, 11) more times—68 (76, 84) stitches.

Slip the first and last stitch from the instep needle back to the heel needle; note that this moves the start of the round by 1 stitch—you will now have 34 (38, 42) stitches on each side.

LEG

The first round begins on the second stitch as the start of the round has been moved.

Work all 68 (76, 84) stitches in right or left leg pattern, as appropriate. Ensure you begin on the correct row of the pattern to maintain instep pattern.

Work in pattern until leg measures 5½ (6, 6½)" (14 [15, 16.5]cm) from start of leg pattern at heel, or desired length.

Cuff Rib: With smaller-size needle, *p2, k2; repeat from * to last 2 stitches, p2.

Work cuff rib for 1" (2.5cm).

Bind off all stitches using elastic bind-off.

FINISHING

Weave in all loose ends. Block sock to dimensions given.

limon

SIDE-TO-SIDE HAT

Knit from side to side, this beret uses slipped stitches and short rows to full effect. The slipped-stitch headband draws the fabric in tightly for a good fit, and the short rows allow the crown of the beret to be shaped without any decreases.

Skill Level Intermediate

Sizes

To fit head circumference up to 20 (22¼, 24½)" (51 [56.5, 62]cm)

2" (5cm) negative ease recommended

Finished Measurements

Hatband circumference: 18 (20¼, 22½)" (45.5 [51.5, 57]cm)

Size 20¼" (51.5cm) modeled with 2" (5cm) of negative ease

Materials

YARN

1 (1, 2) skeins Anzula Cricket, 80% superwash merino, 10% cashmere, 10% nylon, 4 oz (114g), 250 yd (228m), in Avocado 🔲 light

NEEDLES & NOTIONS

1 US size 4 (3.5mm) circular needle, 16" (40.5cm) long

Adjust needle size as necessary to achieve gauge.

US size E-4 (3.5mm) crochet hook for provisional cast-on

Waste yarn for provisional cast-on

Stitch markers

Safety pins or waste yarn for Japanese short rows

Tapestry needle

Gauge

22 stitches and 36 rows = 4" (10cm) in stockinette stitch, blocked

30 stitches and 50 rows = 4" (10cm) in slip stitch pattern, blocked

Short Row Method Used

Japanese (page 14)

Techniques

For other techniques used in the pattern, please refer to General Techniques (page 155).

SLIP STITCH CHART

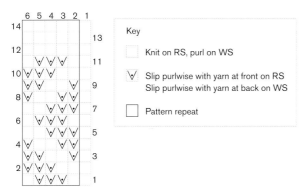

Note: Full written instructions for the chart are given within the pattern.

Pattern Notes

- Do not confuse your slipped stitches. In the slip stitch pattern, the slipped stitch is always worked with the yarn across the right side of the work.
- When you are slipping the Japanese short row, your yarn is on the front side.
- When working several Japanese short rows one after another, I find it's best to use a long piece of yarn instead of safety pins, looping the yarn across the working yarn every time you work a short row.

HAT WEDGE

Note: All stitches are slipped purlwise.

Using provisional cast-on method, cast on 62 (66, 70) stitches. Purl 1 row.

Row 1 (RS): K1, *k1, slip 3 stitches, one at a time, with yarn in front, k1; repeat from * twice more, place marker (slip this marker after first repeat), knit to last stitch, turn work.

Row 2 (WS): Slip stitch, place safety pin, purl to marker, slip marker, *slip 3 stitches with yarn in back, p2; repeat from * twice more, p1.

Row 3 (RS): K1, *slip stitch with yarn in front, k2, slip 2 stitches with yarn in front; repeat from * twice more, slip marker, knit to 1 stitch before gap, turn work.

Row 4 (WS): Slip stitch, place safety pin, purl to marker, slip marker, *slip stitch with yarn in back, p2, slip 2 stitches with yarn in back; repeat from * twice more, p1.

Row 5 (RS): K1, *slip 3 stitches with yarn in front, k2; repeat from * twice more, slip marker, knit to 1 stitch before gap, turn work.

Row 6 (WS): Slip stitch, place safety pin, purl to marker, slip marker, *p1, slip 3 stitches with yarn in back, p1; repeat from * twice more, p1.

Row 7 (RS): K1, *slip 3 stitches with yarn in front, k2; repeat from * twice more, slip marker, knit to 1 stitch before gap, turn work.

Row 8 (WS): Slip stitch, place safety pin, purl to marker, slip marker, *slip stitch with yarn in back, p2, slip 2 stitches with yarn in back; repeat from * twice more, p1.

Row 9 (RS): K1, *slip 1 stitch with yarn in front, k2, slip 2 stitches with yarn in front; repeat from * twice more, slip marker, knit to 1 stitch before gap, turn work.

Row 10 (WS): Slip stitch, place safety pin, purl to marker, slip marker, *slip 3 stitches with yarn in back, p2; repeat from * twice more, p1.

Row 11 (RS): K1, *k1, slip 3 stitches with yarn in front, k1; repeat from * twice more, slip marker, knit to 1 stitch before gap, turn work.

Row 12 (WS): Slip stitch, place safety pin, purl to end of row.

Row 13 (RS): Knit to 1 stitch before gap, turn work.

Row 14 (WS): Slip stitch, place safety pin, purl to end of row.

Row 15 (RS): K1, *k1, slip 3 stitches with yarn in front, k1; repeat from * twice more, slip marker, knit to 1 stitch before gap, turn work.

Rows 16–26: Repeat rows 2–12.

Row 27 (RS): Knit to end of row, working all yarn loops with the corresponding stitch as you pass them.

Row 28 (WS): Slip stitch purlwise with yarn in front, purl to end of row.

Work these 28 rows 7 (8, 9) more times. On the final repeat, omit row 28.

FINISHING

Undo provisional cast-on and place all stitches on needle, ensuring you have 62 (66, 70) stitches. Pick up loop at edge of work to correct stitch count.

With right side facing, graft together all 62 (66, 70) stitches from start and end of hat.

Weave yarn through slip-stitch loops at top of hat and draw together, closing the crown of the hat.

Weave in all loose ends. Block hat, taking care to shape well. A larger bowl or plate is ideal to use as a form to shape the crown of the hat.

zapote
CHILD'S HOODED JACKET

This jacket is knit from the top down using short rows to shape the hood. The shoulders are shaped in one piece with raglan increases, and the body is finished with an A-line shape and garter stitch pockets. I knit this jacket for my niece, and it's one of her mother's favorites!

Skill Level Intermediate

Sizes and Finished Measurements

To fit up to age	months				years			
	6	12	18	2	4	6	8	10
Actual Chest Circumference	19¼" (49cm)	20¾" (52.5cm)	21½" (55cm)	23¼" (59cm)	25½" (65cm)	27¼" (69cm)	28¾" (73cm)	30½" (77.5cm)
Length (omitting hood)	12¼" (31cm)	13¼" (33.5cm)	14¼" (36cm)	15¼" (38.5cm)	16¼" (41.5cm)	16¾" (42.5cm)	17½" (44.5cm)	18¼" (46.5cm)

12-month size modeled on 12-month-old with 2" (5cm) positive ease
18-month size modeled on 18-month-old with 2" (5cm) positive ease

Materials

YARN

12-month size: 2 (3, 3, 3, 4, 4, 5, 5) skeins Fyberspates Vivacious DK, 100% superwash merino, 4 oz (113g), 251 yd (230m), in aqua (807) (4) medium

18-month size: 1 (1, 2, 2, 2, 2, 2, 3) skeins Miss Babs Yowza!, 100% superwash merino, 8 oz (227g), 560 yd (512m), in Coventry (4) medium

NEEDLES & NOTIONS

2 US size 6 (4mm) circular needles, 32" (81cm) long

1 set US size 6 (4mm) double-pointed needles
Adjust needle size as necessary to achieve gauge.
US size G-6 (4mm) crochet hook for provisional cast-on

Waste yarn for provisional cast-on

Stitch markers

(continues)

Tapestry needle

3 (3, 4, 4, 4, 4, 4, 5) toggle buttons, 1" (2.5cm) long

Gauge

20 stitches and 28 rows = 4" (10cm) in stockinette stitch, blocked

20 stitches and 40 rows = 4" (10cm) in garter stitch, blocked

Short Row Method Used

German (page 18)

Techniques

For all other techniques used in the pattern, please refer to General Techniques (page 155).

I-CORD

*Knit 3 stitches, slip 3 stitches just worked to the other end of the double-pointed needle and tug yarn snugly; repeat from * until I-cord is desired length.

Pattern Notes

I recommend placing a safety pin on the right side of the hood to keep track when you are working it in garter stitch.

HOOD

Left Side

With circular needle and waste yarn, cast on 39 (40, 42, 43, 46, 48, 49, 52) stitches using provisional cast-on.

Setup Row (WS): With working yarn, knit to last 3 stitches, slip 3 stitches purlwise with yarn in front.

Short Row 1 (RS): Knit 23 (22, 22, 23, 24, 24, 23, 24) stitches, turn work.

Next row (WS): Slip 1 stitch purlwise with yarn in front, pull yarn over needle (*creating double stitch*), knit to last 3 stitches, slip 3 stitches purlwise.

Short Row 2 (RS): Knit to double stitch, knit double stitch together as 1 stitch, k2, turn work.

Repeat these last 2 rows until all stitches have been worked. Work 1 more wrong-side row.

Next row (RS): Knit all stitches (*including final double stitch*), place marker, undo provisional cast-on, placing resultant 39 (40, 42, 43, 46, 48, 49, 52) stitches on a 2nd circular needle ready to work, knit these stitches to last 3 stitches, slip 3 stitches purlwise with yarn in front.

Right Side

Short Row 1 (WS): K23 (22, 22, 23, 24, 24, 23, 24) stitches, turn work.

Next row (RS): Slip 1 stitch purlwise with yarn in front, pull yarn over needle (*creating double stitch*), knit to last 3 stitches, slip 3 stitches purlwise.

Short Row 2 (WS): Knit to double stitch, knit double stitch together as 1 stitch, k2, turn work.

Repeat these last 2 rows until all stitches have been worked. Work 1 more right-side row.

Complete Hood

Note: It may be necessary to continue using 2 circular needles when you start working the complete hood. Switch to a single circular needle when it is comfortable to do so.

Full Hood Row (WS): Knit to last 3 stitches, slip 3 stitches purlwise—78 (80, 84, 86, 92, 96, 98, 104) stitches.

Note: This row establishes the pattern for the hood.

Work in pattern for 4 (4, 6, 6, 6, 8, 12, 16) more rows, ending with a wrong-side row.

Dec Row (RS): Knit to 4 stitches before marker, k2tog, k2, slip marker, k2, ssk, knit to last 3 stitches, slip 3 stitches purlwise—76 (78, 82, 84, 90, 94, 96, 102) stitches; 2 stitches decreased.

Work dec row every 6 (6, 8, 8, 8, 8, 14, 16) rows 5 (3, 1, 5, 5, 7, 2, 3) times and then every 4 (4, 6, 6, 6, −, 12, −) rows 5 (8, 7, 2, 3, −, 2, −) times—56 (56, 66, 70, 74, 80, 88, 96) stitches.

Remove marker.

Work 6 (6, 8, 10, 8, 10, 14, 18) rows even in pattern, ending with a right-side row.

YOKE

Raglan Setup Row (WS): K9 (9, 11, 11, 11, 13, 13, 13), place marker, p6 (6, 6, 7, 8, 8, 9, 10), place marker, p4 (4, 6, 6, 6, 6, 8, 10), place marker, p18 (18, 20, 22, 24, 26, 28, 30), place marker, p4 (4, 6, 6, 6, 6, 8, 10), place marker, p6 (6, 6, 7, 8, 8, 9, 10), place marker, k6 (6, 8, 8, 8, 10, 10, 10), slip 3 stitches purlwise with yarn in front.

Raglan Inc Row (RS): Knit to marker, slip marker, *knit to last stitch before marker, kfb, slip marker, kfb; repeat from * 3 more times, knit to last 3 stitches, slip 3 stitches purlwise with yarn in front—8 stitches increased.

Next row (WS): Knit to first marker, slip marker, purl to final marker, slip marker, knit to final 3 stitches, slip 3 stitches purlwise with yarn in front.

Repeat these 2 rows 14 (16, 16, 17, 19, 20, 21, 22) more times—176 (192, 202, 214, 234, 248, 264, 280) stitches; 30 (32, 34, 36, 39, 42, 44, 46) stitches each front, 34 (38, 40, 42, 46, 48, 52, 56) stitches each sleeve, 48 (52, 54, 58, 64, 68, 72, 76) back stitches.

Work 2 (0, 2, 4, 4, 6, 6, 6) rows even in pattern.

BODY

Sleeve Divide Row (RS): Work in pattern to second marker, *remove marker, slip next 34 (38, 40, 42, 46, 48, 52, 56) stitches onto waste yarn, slip marker*, knit back stitches to next marker, repeat from * to *, work in pattern to end of row—108 (116, 122, 130, 142, 152, 160, 168) stitches.

Next row (WS): Knit to marker, purl to marker, knit to last 3 stitches, slip 3 stitches purlwise with yarn in front.

Work even in pattern for 8 rows.

Body Inc Row (RS): *Knit to 1 stitch before side marker, M1R, k1, slip marker, k1, M1L; repeat from * once more, work in pattern to end of row—112 (120, 126, 134, 146, 156, 164, 172) stitches; 4 stitches increased.

Work 1 wrong-side row.

Pockets
Both pockets will be worked at the same time with 2 separate balls of yarn. Instructions for each side of the pocket are divided by a semicolon.

Slip first and last 15 (15, 17, 17, 18, 20, 21, 21) stitches onto a second circular needle; these stitches will form the pockets and are worked first. Use original circular needle as holder for remaining 82 (90, 92, 100, 110, 116, 122, 130) stitches; these stitches will form the body and are worked later.

Next row (RS): Knit left-hand side; with 2nd ball of yarn, knit to last 3 stitches, slip 3 stitches purlwise with yarn in front.

Next row (WS): Knit right-hand side; knit to last 3 stitches, slip 3 stitches purlwise with yarn in front.

Work in pattern established for 8 (8, 8, 10, 10, 12, 12, 14) more rows.

Inc Row (RS): Knit to last stitch of left pocket, M1L, k1; k1, M1R, knit to last 3 stitches, slip 3 stitches purlwise with yarn in front—1 stitch increased each side.

Work wrong-side row as before.

Repeat these 2 rows 1 (1, 1, 1, 2, 2, 2, 3) more times—17 (17, 19, 19, 21, 23, 24, 25) stitches each side.

Work right-side inc row once more.

Inc Row (WS): Knit to last stitch on right pocket, M1L, k1; k1 M1R, knit to last 3 stitches, slip 3 stitches purlwise with yarn in front—1 stitch increased each side.

Repeat these 2 rows twice more—23 (23, 25, 25, 27, 29, 30, 31) stitches each side.

Cast-On Row (RS): Work left pocket in pattern; cast on 6 (6, 8, 8, 8, 8, 9, 10) stitches using cable cast-on, work in pattern to end of row.

Cast-On Row (WS): Work right pocket in pattern; cast on 6 (6, 8, 8, 8, 8, 9, 10) stitches using cable cast-on, work in pattern to end of row—29 (29, 33, 33, 35, 37, 39, 41) stitches each side.

Work even in pattern until pocket measures 4¼ (4¾, 5¼, 5¼, 5¾, 5¾, 6, 6½)" (11 [12, 13.5, 13.5, 14.5, 14.5, 15, 16.5]cm) from the top of the pocket, ending with a wrong-side row.

Set these stitches aside until the joining row.

Lower Body
Reattach yarn to 82 (90, 92, 100, 110, 116, 122, 130) stitches held on first needle.

Cast-On Row (RS): Cast on 6 (6, 6, 6, 7, 7, 8, 8) stitches using cable cast-on, knit to end of row.

Cast-On Row (WS): Cast on 6 (6, 6, 6, 7, 7, 8, 8) stitches using cable cast-on, purl to end of row—94 (102, 104, 112, 124, 130, 138, 146) stitches.

Work 8 rows in stockinette stitch.

Work body inc row.

Continue to work in stockinette stitch, working body inc row every 12 rows 1 (1, 2, 2, 2, 2, 2, 3) more time(s)—102 (110, 116, 124, 136, 142, 150, 162) stitches.

Work even in stockinette until work measures the same length as the pockets, ending with a wrong-side row.

Joining Row (RS): Working on left pocket, k9 (9, 11, 11, 11, 13, 13, 13), holding body needle parallel to and behind pocket, *knit 1 stitch from pocket and 1 stitch from body together; repeat from * until all pocket stitches have been worked, knit to last 20 (20, 22, 22, 24, 24, 26, 28) body stitches, holding body needle parallel to and behind pocket, *knit 1 stitch from pocket and 1 stitch from body together; repeat from * until all body stitches have been worked, knit to last 3 pocket stitches, slip 3 stitches purlwise with yarn in front—120 (128, 138, 146, 158, 168, 176, 188) stitches.

Edging
Next row (WS): Knit to to last 3 stitches, slip 3 stitches purlwise with yarn in front.

Next row (RS): Knit to to last 3 stitches, slip 3 stitches purlwise with yarn in front.

Work in pattern until edging measures 1¾ (2, 2, 2½, 2½, 2½, 2½, 2½)" (4.5 [5, 5, 6.5, 6.5, 6.5, 6.5, 6.5]cm), ending with a wrong-side row.

Work 2 rows of unattached I-cord on the first 3 stitches to create corner of cardigan.

Bind off to last 3 stitches using I-cord bind-off, using first 3 stitches of row as the start of your I-cord bind-off.

Graft together the 3 I-cord stitches with the 3 stitches unworked on left needle to form a seamless I-cord edge.

SLEEVES
Evenly divide the held 34 (38, 40, 42, 46, 48, 52, 56) sleeve stitches on double-pointed needles. Join to work in the round.

Knit 9 (8, 9, 12, 12, 14, 12, 9) rounds.

Sleeve Dec Rnd: K2tog, work to last 2 stitches, ssk—32 (36, 38, 40, 44, 46, 50, 54) stitches; 2 stitches decreased.

Repeat these 10 (9, 10, 13, 13, 15, 13, 10) rounds 2 (3, 3, 2, 3, 3, 4, 6) more times—28 (30, 32, 36, 38, 40, 42, 42) stitches.

Work even in stockinette stitch until sleeve measures 5 (6, 6½, 7, 8½, 9½, 10½, 11)" (12.5 [15, 16.5, 18, 21.5, 24, 26.5, 28]cm) from armhole or desired length.

Work in garter stitch for 1½ (1½, 1½, 2, 2, 2, 2, 2½)" (3.8 [3.8, 3.8, 5, 5, 5, 5, 6.5]cm). Bind off all stitches using I-cord bind-off (casting on 3 stitches for I-cord at beginning).

FINISHING

I-Cord Buttonholes

Using double-pointed needles, cast on 3 stitches.

*Knit all stitches, slip all stitches to right-hand end of needle, pull yarn snugly to close gap; repeat from * until I-cord measures approximately 4 (4, 5, 5, 5, 6, 6, 6)" (10 [10, 12.5, 12.5, 12.5, 15, 15, 15]cm). **Note:** *Work longer or shorter I-cord if you are using larger or smaller buttons.* Bind off all stitches.

Repeat this 2 (2, 3, 3, 3, 3, 3, 4) more times or for desired number of buttonholes.

Fold I-cord in half and pin ends in position on right-hand side of front for girl, left-hand side for boy. *In sample, 3" (7.5cm) spacing between buttonholes is used.*

Sew I-cord carefully in place with yarn and tapestry needle. Sew buttons in position opposite I-cord buttonholes.

Sew pockets neatly in position.

Weave in all loose ends.

Block garment to dimensions given in schematic.

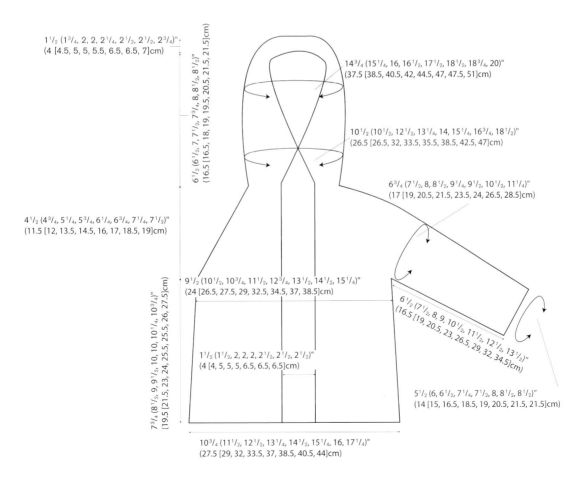

3

short rows
IN GARMENTS

Barbara Walker's book *Knitting from the Top* (Schoolhouse Press, 1972) really opened my eyes to the many different ways that short rows can be used to create well-fitted garments. They can fix many common problems, such as stair-step shoulder bind-offs, hip curves, and bust shaping. This chapter is not a definitive list, but rather a good starting point to thinking about how you can incorporate short rows into your knitting. Once you've grasped the concepts, you'll find that many techniques can be incorporated into other patterns—originally designed without short rows—for a much-improved fit.

Raising the Back of the Neck

When a pattern is worked seamlessly (either bottom up or top down), the easiest way to ensure that the back of the neck is raised higher than the front is by working short rows. These short rows add only a small amount of extra height at the back of the neck, but they make a considerable difference in how well a garment fits. This technique is most commonly used for circular-yoke garments that are knit seamlessly. Without the short rows, there would be no difference between the back and front of the garment.

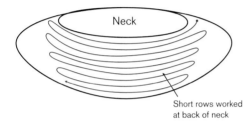

Short rows worked
at back of neck

In the example above, you can see that the short rows are worked across the back of the neck, starting at the back of the neck (as pictured) and working down so they step in at each side every time you turn. This doesn't work for all patterns though; sometimes it fits into the design better if the short rows are worked farther down the yoke on the back (such as for a colorwork yoke). It's even possible to work half the short rows at the bottom of the yoke and the other half at the top.

If you work the short rows all the way to the front of the neck, you can even create a curved neckline shape. With this technique, the short rows become almost an extension of the back neck shaping.

Typically, you will begin your short rows at the center of each shoulder, working a short row at each side. If you're working from the top down, for the next set of short rows, work ½" (13mm) fewer stitches than the previous short rows. Continue working short rows inward until approximately 1" (2.5cm) of short rows have been worked. If you are working from the bottom up, you will reverse the way the short rows are worked, working from the narrowest to the widest point.

Creating Shoulder Slopes

For a standard set-in-sleeve garment that is knit flat in pieces, the tops of the shoulders are sloped using a series of bind-off rows. This can be replaced with a series of short rows to create a smooth slope that can be joined afterward using a three-needle bind-off at the shoulder.

SHORT ROW SHOULDER

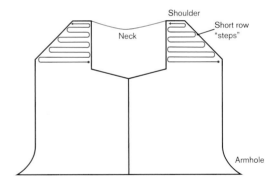

converting standard patterns

With a standard pattern worked in flat pieces from the bottom up, the shoulder will be shaped by binding off stitches at the start of each row until all shoulder stitches are bound off. This creates a shoulder slope with a "stair-step" effect.

STANDARD "STAIR-STEP" SHOULDERS

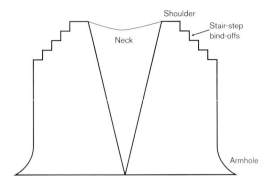

It is very simple to convert this to short rows. Knit straight until the last two rows of armhole length you need. Every time the pattern says to bind off stitches, work a short row instead. When you have finished, you won't have the "stair steps"; instead you will have a smooth short-row slope! The final step is to work across the final right- and wrong-side rows to pick up all of the short-row wraps; this is why you allowed those extra two rows in your knitted length.

If you work this method on both the front and back of your work, all your stitches will be live, so you can use a three-needle bind-off (page 157) instead of seaming the shoulders. This gives a wonderfully professional finish that's really easy to work.

adjusting shoulder slope

Not everyone's shoulders slope at the same angle. Take a look at your shoulders in the mirror. Are they very straight and square, or do they slope at a steep angle? Using short rows you can create a slope to suit your body shape.

For a standard shoulder slope, Barbara Walker suggests working the short rows at ¾" (2cm) intervals. However, if you have very square shoulders, you will want a flatter shoulder slope. In the previous section, we showed how adjusting the stitches between short rows changes the slope of your knitting. So to create a flatter

slope, you will want to work more spaces between your short row turns, perhaps at 1" (2.5cm) intervals.

The opposite is true if you have sloped shoulders. You will want a steeper slope, so you need to move your short row steps closer together, perhaps working your short row turns every ½" (13mm) instead.

Shaping Hems

The hem of garments can also be shaped using short rows. This shaping can be very subtle to create a gentle curve, or very dramatic. You can even create an asymmetrical hemline by working short rows at one side only.

Short rows can also be added at the hem to correct fit issues. If the garment is pulling up at the front or at the back, a small number of short rows at the hem will help it lie flat across the hem.

SHORT ROW HEM CURVE

To create a curved hem at the back of a garment, I recommend working through the steps outlined for shaping a shawl in the last chapter (page 46). Sketch the shape you would like, then calculate the number of short rows you need in total and the stitches between each turn. Remember that you can adjust the number of stitches between the turns as you go to create a more complex curve.

Working from Side to Side

Garments look completely different when they are knit from side to side. This works especially well with self-striping yarn as you turn horizontal stripes into vertical stripes.

In order to shape the body of a sideways-knit garment, you need to add short rows at the hips to create an A-line shape. The overall width at the hips is determined by the number of short rows that you add.

SHORT ROW HIP SHAPING

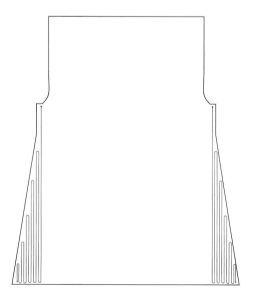

You can see how the addition of short rows creates a wider hip than bust. In the first example, all of the short rows are added at the side. This can be useful if you want to keep a large stitch pattern uninterrupted.

However, these short rows can also be distributed at different places around the garment for a more subtle effect. Often I will divide the total number of short rows by four, adding one-fourth to each side of the center, and one-fourth to each side of the body.

DISTRIBUTED SHORT ROW HIP SHAPING

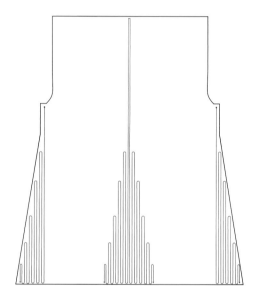

Creating Set-In Sleeves

Set-in sleeves are one of the most useful applications of short rows. Standard set-in sleeves are sewn into the body and can be tricky to ease into position. In order to create the correct shape, the armhole and sleeve cap are knit to the same overall lengths but are different shapes. The sleeve cap then has to be eased into place as you are seaming, which takes time and a lot of patience! To create a short row sleeve-cap with much less effort, pick up stitches around the armhole and work a series of short rows across the armhole opening.

SET-IN SLEEVE

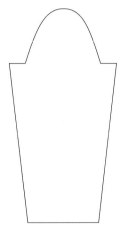

SHORT ROW SLEEVE CAP

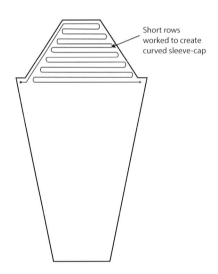

Short rows worked to create curved sleeve-cap

set-in sleeve technique

Begin by picking up sleeve stitches (as many as needed for the top of the sleeve) around the armhole, starting at the center bottom. Take care that there are the same number of stitches at each side. You will notice that the pick-up rate is quite different from the standard: it will be almost one stitch for every two rows. Next, mark off the central third of the stitches, centered at the top of the shoulder. Work to the end of this marked top third (two-thirds of total stitches) and work your first short row. When you turn to the wrong side, work the top third of the stitches and then work your next short row. After these first two short rows, continue to work to the previous turn, work one extra stitch, and then work another short row. Keep working back and forth in this way until you reach the underarm stitches and then begin working the sleeve in the round.

As you can see, this type of sleeve cap is not a perfect curve like the sewn set-in sleeve cap; it has a flat top and straight sides. Thanks to the flexible nature of the knitted fabric, however, it curves beautifully to form a perfect cap.

The "top-third rule" works for most knitted fabrics, but sometimes it may be necessary to make some adjustments. For a chunky yarn, you may find that you don't have enough rows for the number of short row stitches. In this case, you can use less than a third of the stitches at the center to make more stitches available to work short rows at each side. Don't work short rows into the underarm; you don't want your sleeve cap curving right into your armpit!

Shaping Bust Darts

There are two types of darts you can add at the bust: vertical or horizontal. When working from the bottom, vertical darts are worked as increases coming up to the bust and as decreases after the bust; these add extra width at the bust. Horizontal darts are worked as a series of short rows at the bust area, and they add extra length to the front of a garment at the bust.

I will focus on horizontal darts in this book. It's important to note that short-row horizontal bust darts only add
length to the garment, not extra width. However, for many
women, this adds enough extra fabric to stop a garment
from pulling at the bust and allows it to fit the body better.
On the next page I show a series of calculations that you
can use to decide how much length you need to add to
the bust area.

SHORT ROW BUST SHAPING

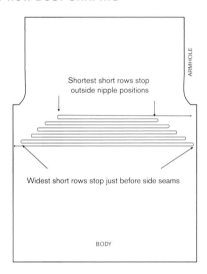

Shortest short rows stop
outside nipple positions

ARMHOLE

Widest short rows stop just before side seams

BODY

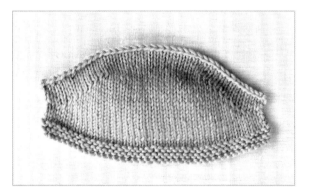

You can see in the diagram above how the short row
shaping will look in the bust. In this swatch, the short
rows are worked every stitch, which creates a dramatic

dart line at the side of the bust. The farther apart the short
rows are spaced, the subtler the effect will be.

Not all bust sizes will need short row bust darts.
When you measure yourself, if the difference between the
front and back lengths is less than 3" (7.5cm), you don't
need to add any short row darts. For length differences
greater than this, you can add extra length, but use about
2" (5cm) of negative ease to allow for the fact that the
knitted fabric stretches in length when it is worn. This
will also help prevent a gathered pocket of fabric from
forming at the bust area.

In the patterns written for this chapter, I provide
three bust dart sizes, which add 2 (3, 4)" (5 [7.5, 10]cm)
of length. These are suitable for front and back length
differences (see measurement C, opposite) up to 4 (5,
6)" (10, [12.5, 15]cm). If you need a different number of
short rows, the guidance provided here could be used to
make the adjustment.

EASE

The term *ease* is used to describe how a garment
fits your body. If a garment is made to the exact
body measurement, it has no ease. If it is made
larger than the body measurement it has positive
ease. If it is made smaller than the body measurement it has negative ease. For the purposes
of this book we are just referring to the ease at
the bust but it can be used with any other body
measurement.

If you use very little or no ease, the garment will
be very fitted when worn. Most garments are
knitted with a little bit of positive ease for a more
relaxed fit.

In terms of positioning short rows, if you are working from the bottom up, begin them 2 (3, 4)" (5 [7.5, 10]cm) below the fullest bust point. Working from the top down, begin the short rows at the fullest bust point.

To position the short rows in your garment, start a little in from the side seam and stop just outside your nipple (approximately 1" [2.5cm] out each side). The number of stitches in each row will depend on the number of rows and your gauge.

short row bust-shaping calculations

You can use this worksheet to calculate the number of short rows you need for bust shaping in any pattern.

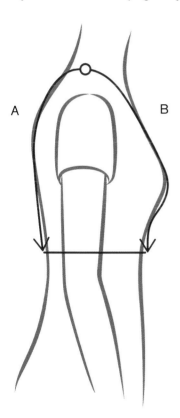

A. Length from shoulder to under bust at back = _____ inches (cm)

B. Length from shoulder to under bust at front over bust = _____ inches (cm)

C. B − A = _____ inches (cm)

D. C x rows per inch (cm) = _____ rows (*Remember that every time we work a short row, it takes up two rows, forward and back.*)

E. D ÷ 2 = _____ turns each side

This is the number of *turns* we have at each side of our bust. You can make small adjustments to the number here to ensure you have an even number of turns on each side.

Number of stitches each side for short rows:

F. Width of your garment = _____ inches (cm)

G. Nipple to nipple = _____ inches (cm)

Note that we start the short rows at least 1" (2.5cm) outside this point on each side; this is added below.

H. (F − G − 2" [5cm]) ÷ 2 = _____ inches (cm) each side of body to work short rows

I. H x stitches per inch (cm) = _____ stitches

This is the number of stitches we have on each side to work our short rows.

J. I / E = _____ stitches between each turn.

Adjust this number as necessary so that you don't have a fraction of a stitch.

So we will work E short rows on each side of J stitches.

> **Note:** If your number is uneven, you can vary the rate that the short rows are worked or you can add the extra stitches at the side or center.

COLORWORK YOKE SWEATER

The geometric colorwork yoke of this sweater, which is worked from the bottom up in one piece, makes a striking statement. The neck is delicately shaped by working short rows across the back to raise it. This makes the sweater more comfortable to wear as it keeps the back of your neck warm and prevents the front from pulling up too high under your chin. This technique can be used to modify any sweater that you wish, either seamed or seamless.

Skill Level Intermediate

Sizes and Finished Measurements

To Fit Bust Circumference (up to)	31" (79cm)	34½" (87.5cm)	37¼" (94.5cm)	40" (101.5cm)	43½" (110.5cm)	46" (117cm)	49¾" (126.5cm)	52¼" (132.5cm)	55" (140cm)
Bust Size	32" (81cm)	35½" (90cm)	38¼" (97cm)	41" (104cm)	44½" (113cm)	47" (119.5cm)	50¾" (129cm)	53¼" (135.5cm)	56" (142cm)
Length	21¾" (55.5cm)	22" (56cm)	22¼" (56.5cm)	22¾" (58cm)	23¼" (59cm)	23¼" (59cm)	23¾" (60cm)	24¼" (61.5cm)	24½" (62cm)

Size 35½" (90cm) modeled with 1" (2.5cm) of positive ease

Materials

YARN
Harrisville Designs WATERshed, 100% wool, 1.75 oz (50g), 110 yd (101m), 8 (9, 9, 10, 10, 11, 12, 12, 13) skeins in 909 Bancroft (MC), 1 skein in 919 Canal (CC1), and 1 skein in 931 Eastview (CC2) 🔒 medium

NEEDLES & NOTIONS
1 US size 7 (4.5mm) circular needle, 32" (81cm) long, for body (or longer for larger sizes)
1 US size 7 (4.5mm) circular needle, 24" (61cm) long, for neck
Set of US size 7 (4.5mm) double-pointed needles for sleeves

(continues)

Adjust needle size as necessary to achieve gauge.

Stitch markers

Stitch holders or waste yarn

Tapestry needle

Gauge

18 stitches and 24 rows = 4" (10cm) in stockinette stitch, blocked

19 stitches and 24 rows = 4" (10cm) in ribbing, lightly blocked

Short Row Method Used

Wrap and Turn (page 10)

Techniques

For other techniques used in the pattern, please refer to General Techniques (page 155).

YOKE CHART

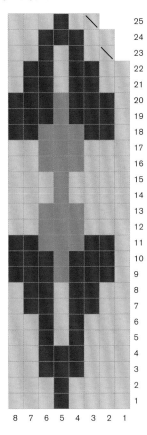

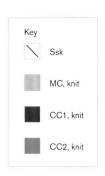

Key

⟋ Ssk

▢ MC, knit

■ CC1, knit

▨ CC2, knit

Pattern Notes

Short rows are worked at the neck of this sweater to raise the back of the neck up. Wrap-and-turn short rows have been used, but you can also substitute your preferred short row method.

BODY

Using longer circular needle and MC, cast on 144 (160, 172, 184, 200, 212, 228, 240, 252) stitches. Place marker for start of round and join to work in the round.

Ribbing Rnd: *K2, p2; repeat from * to end of round.

Repeat this round until ribbing measures 2" (5cm).

Placing Marker Rnd: K36 (40, 43, 46, 50, 53, 57, 60, 63), place marker for side seam, k72 (80, 86, 92, 100, 106, 114, 120, 126), place marker for side seam, knit to end of round.

Pocket Divide Rnd: Knit to side marker, slip marker, k16 (19, 22, 23, 27, 29, 33, 35, 38), with second (shorter) circular needle k40 (42, 42, 46, 46, 48, 48, 50, 50); remaining 104 (118, 130, 138, 154, 164, 180, 190, 202) stitches will be held on first needle until the front of pocket has been worked.

Work 40 (42, 42, 46, 46, 48, 48, 50, 50) pocket stitches flat in stockinette stitch for 27 rows, ending with a wrong-side row. Break yarn, set pocket stitches aside.

For back of pocket, with right side facing, rejoin yarn to remaining 104 (118, 130, 138, 154, 164, 180, 190, 202) stitches at left side of pocket; using backward-loop cast-on, cast on 40 (42, 42, 46, 46, 48, 48, 50, 50) stitches, join to work in round; knit to end of round—144 (160, 172, 184, 200, 212, 228, 240, 252) body stitches, 40 (42, 42, 46, 46, 48, 48, 50, 50) held pocket stitches.

Waist Dec Rnd: *Knit to 4 stitches before side marker, ssk, k2, slip marker, k2, k2tog; repeat from * once more—140 (156, 168, 180, 196, 208, 224, 236, 248) stitches; 4 stitches decreased.

Work waist dec rnd every 5 rounds 3 more times—128 (144, 156, 168, 184, 196, 212, 224, 236) stitches.

Knit 12 rounds even in stockinette stitch.

Pocket Joining Rnd: Knit to side marker, slip marker, k12 (15, 18, 19, 23, 25, 29, 31, 34), holding pocket stitches to front, *k2tog using 1 stitch from front needle and 1 stitch from back needle; repeat from * until all 40 (42, 42, 46, 46, 48, 48, 50, 50) pocket stitches have been joined, knit to end of round.

Bust Inc Rnd: *Knit to 2 stitches before side marker, M1R, k2, slip marker, k2, M1L; repeat from * once more—132 (148, 160, 172, 188, 200, 216, 228, 240) stitches; 4 stitches increased.

Work bust inc rnd every 9 (9, 9, 9, 10, 10, 10, 10, 10) rounds 3 more times—144 (160, 172, 184, 200, 212, 228, 240, 252) stitches.

Work even in stockinette stitch until body measures 14 (14, 14, 14, 14¼, 14¼, 14½, 14½, 14½)" (35.5 [35.5, 35.5, 35.5, 36, 36, 37, 37, 37]cm) from bottom of hem.

Set stitches aside but do not break yarn.

SLEEVES
Using double-pointed needles, cast on 40 (40, 40, 40, 44, 44, 44, 48, 48) stitches, place marker for start of round and join to work in round.

Rib Rnd: *K2, p2; repeat from * to end of round.

Work rib rnd until work measures 2" (5cm).

Work in stockinette stitch for 12 (11, 10, 8, 10, 8, 6, 6, 5) rounds.

Inc Rnd: K1, M1L, knit to last st, M1R, k1—2 stitches increased.

Repeat these 13 (12, 11, 9, 11, 9, 7, 7, 6) rounds 5 (6, 7, 9, 7, 9, 11, 12, 14) more times—52 (54, 56, 60, 60, 64, 68, 74, 78) stitches.

Work even in stockinette stitch until sleeve measures 18 (18½, 18½, 18½, 19, 19, 19, 19½, 19½)" (45.5 [47, 47, 47, 48.5, 48.5, 48.5, 49.5, 49.5]cm) from cast-on or desired length.

Place 2 (4, 6, 7, 8, 10, 12, 13, 14) stitches from start and end of round on waste yarn—48 (46, 44, 46, 44, 44, 44, 48, 50) stitches.

Set stitches aside on holder or waste yarn and break working yarn.

Repeat for second sleeve.

YOKE

Underarm Rnd: With circular needle, using working yarn attached to body, *knit to 2 (4, 6, 7, 8, 10, 12, 13, 14) stitches before side marker, slip next 4 (8, 12, 14, 16, 20, 24, 26, 28) stitches onto waste yarn, place raglan marker, k48 (46, 44, 46, 44, 44, 44, 48, 50) sleeve stitches, place raglan marker; repeat from * once, knit to end of round—232 (236, 236, 248, 256, 260, 268, 284, 296) stitches total; 48 (46, 44, 46, 44, 44, 44, 48, 50) sleeve stitches, 68 (72, 74, 78, 84, 86, 90, 94, 98) stitches front and back.

Raglan Dec Rnd: *Knit to 2 stitches before raglan marker, k2tog, slip marker, ssk; repeat from * 3 more times, knit to end of round—224 (228, 228, 240, 248, 252, 260, 276, 288) stitches; 8 stitches decreased.

Knit 1 round even.

Repeat these 2 rounds 4 (3, 3, 3, 4, 4, 3, 5, 6) more times—192 (204, 204, 216, 216, 220, 236, 236, 240) stitches.

Remove all raglan markers but leave start-of-round marker in place.

SIZES 32 (35½, 38¼, 41, 44½, –, 50¾, 53¼, –)" (81.5 [90, 97, 104, 113, –, 129, 135.5, –]CM) ONLY
Dec Rnd 1: [K2tog, k94 (49, 49, 34, 34, –, 37, 37, –)] 2 (4, 4, 6, 6, 0, 6, 6, 0) times, knit to end of round if necessary—190 (200, 200, 210, 210, 220, 230, 230, 240) stitches.

ALL SIZES
Knit 5 (10, 12, 13, 13, 15, 17, 15, 17) rounds even.

Dec Rnd 2: [K2tog, k3] 38 (40, 40, 42, 42, 44, 46, 46, 48) times—152 (160, 160, 168, 168, 176, 184, 184, 192) stitches.

Knit 1 round even.

Colorwork Rnd: Work 8-stitch yoke chart (page 98) 19 (20, 20, 21, 21, 22, 23, 23, 24) times to end of round.

Continue to work all 25 rounds of yoke chart until complete—114 (120, 120, 126, 126, 132, 138, 138, 144) stitches.

Notes: Some knitters find that their gauge is tighter when working stranded colorwork. If this is the case for you, I would suggest using a larger needle size for the colorwork.

When working yoke, switch to shorter circular needle when there are too few stitches to fit on the longer needle.

With MC, knit 1 round even.

Neck
Short Row 1 (RS): K33 (34, 34, 36, 36, 38, 39, 39, 41), w&t.

Short Row 2 (WS): P66 (68, 68, 72, 72, 76, 78, 78, 82), w&t.

Short Row 3 (RS): Knit to 3 stitches before previously wrapped stitch, w&t.

Short Row 4 (WS): Purl to 3 stitches before previously wrapped stitch, w&t.

Work short rows 3 and 4 once more.

Next rnd: *Knit to wrapped stitch, work loop with stitch it wraps; repeat from * until all gaps have been closed, knit to end of round.

SIZES 32 (–, –, 41, 44½, –, 50¾, 53¼, –)" (81 [–, –, 104, 113, –, 129, 135.5, –]CM) ONLY
Ribbing Dec Rnd: [K2tog, k55 (–, –, 61, 61, –, 67, 67, –)] twice.

ALL SIZES

Neck Ribbing Rnd: *K2, p2; repeat from * to end of round—112 (120, 120, 124, 124, 132, 136, 136, 144) stitches.

Work neck ribbing rnd 5 more times.

Bind off all stitches loosely in pattern.

FINISHING

Sew bottom of pocket back in position, taking care that it can't be seen from the front.

I-Cord Pocket Edging

With right side facing, using CC1 and circular needle, pick up and knit 3 stitches for every 4 rows along the

edge of the pocket. Break yarn. Slip stitches to other end, rejoin yarn, work I-cord bind-off.

Repeat for the second side of pocket.

Graft underarm stitches from sleeve and body together at each side of the body for a seamless underarm.

Note: There is sometimes a gap at each side of the stitches; this can be closed by either picking up extra stitches to graft or by sewing the gap together.

Weave in all loose ends. Block garment to dimensions given on schematic.

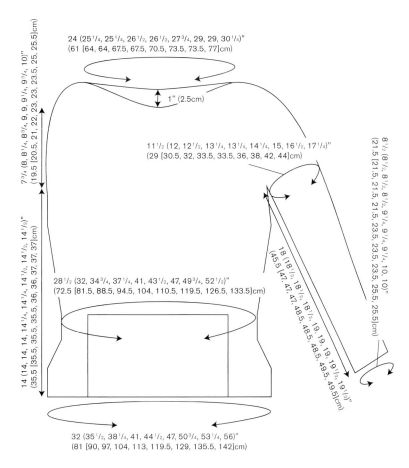

24 (25 1/4, 25 1/4, 26 1/2, 26 1/2, 27 3/4, 29, 29, 30 1/4)"
(61 [64, 64, 67.5, 67.5, 70.5, 73.5, 73.5, 77]cm)

1" (2.5cm)

7 3/4 (8, 8 1/4, 8 3/4, 9, 9, 9 1/4, 9 3/4, 10)"
(19.5 [20.5, 21, 22, 23, 23, 23.5, 25, 25.5]cm)

11 1/2 (12, 12 1/2, 13 1/4, 13 1/4, 14 1/4, 15, 16 1/2, 17 1/4)"
(29 [30.5, 32, 33.5, 33.5, 36, 38, 42, 44]cm)

8 1/2 (8 1/2, 8 1/2, 8 1/2, 9 1/4, 9 1/4, 9 1/4, 10, 10)"
(21.5 [21.5, 21.5, 21.5, 23.5, 23.5, 23.5, 25.5, 25.5]cm)

14 (14, 14, 14, 14 1/4, 14 1/4, 14 1/2, 14 1/2, 14 1/2)"
(35.5 [35.5, 35.5, 35.5, 36, 36, 37, 37, 37]cm)

28 1/2 (32, 34 3/4, 37 1/4, 41, 43 1/2, 47, 49 3/4, 52 1/2)"
(72.5 [81.5, 88.5, 94.5, 104, 110.5, 119.5, 126.5, 133.5]cm)

18 (18 1/2, 18 1/2, 18 1/2, 19, 19, 19, 19 1/2, 19 1/2)"
(45.5 [47, 47, 47, 48.5, 48.5, 48.5, 49.5, 49.5]cm)

32 (35 1/2, 38 1/4, 41, 44 1/2, 47, 50 3/4, 53 1/4, 56)"
(81 [90, 97, 104, 113, 119.5, 129, 135.5, 142]cm)

Note: 1" (2.5cm) neck ribbing is not included in this schematic.

tamarindo
RAGLAN WATERFALL CARDIGAN

This lace-weight cardigan adds a delicate layer of warmth to anything you wear. Knit from the top down, it has wide front panels that can be allowed to drape open or fastened with a shawl pin. Short rows are worked across the back of the neck to gently raise it up for a better fit.

Skill Level Intermediate

Sizes and Finished Measurements

To Fit Bust Circumference (up to)	30" (76cm)	32¾" (83cm)	36" (91cm)	38¾" (98.5cm)	42" (106.5cm)	44¾" (113.5cm)	48" (122cm)	50¾" (129cm)	54" (137cm)
Back Width	15" (38cm)	16¼" (41.5cm)	18" (45.5cm)	19¼" (49cm)	21" (53.5cm)	22¼" (56.5cm)	24" (61cm)	25¼" (64cm)	27" (68.5cm)
Bust Size	30" (76cm)	32¾" (83cm)	36" (91cm)	38¾" (98.5cm)	42" (106.5cm)	44¾" (113.5cm)	48" (122cm)	50¾" (129cm)	54" (137cm)
Length	21½" (55cm)	22" (56cm)	22½" (57cm)	22¾" (58cm)	23" (58.5cm)	23¼" (59cm)	23½" (59.5cm)	23¾" (60.5cm)	24½" (62cm)

Size 36" (91cm) modeled with 1" (2.5cm) of positive ease

Materials

YARN

2 (2, 2, 2, 2, 3, 3, 3) skeins Blue Moon Fiber Arts Laci, 100% extra fine merino, 4 oz (113g), 900 yds (823m), in Ursula (**1**) super fine

NEEDLES & NOTIONS

1 US size 6 (4mm) circular needle, 40" (101.5cm) long (or longer for larger cardigan size)
1 set US size 6 (4mm) double-pointed needles (if Magic Loop is not used for sleeves)

(continues)

NEEDLES & NOTIONS (continued)

Adjust needle size as necessary to achieve gauge.

Stitch markers

Safety pins for Japanese short rows

Waste yarn

Tapestry needle

Gauge

24 stitches and 36 rows = 4" (10cm) in stockinette stitch, blocked

19 stitches and 36 rows = 4" (10 cm) in lace pattern, blocked

Short Row Method Used

Japanese (page 14)

Techniques

For other techniques used in the pattern, please refer to General Techniques (page 155).

LACE CHART

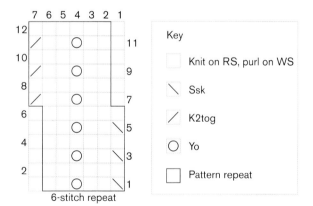

6-stitch repeat

LACE PATTERN

(MULTIPLE OF 6 STITCHES PLUS 1)

Rows 1, 3, and 5 (RS): *Ssk, k2, yo, k2; repeat from * to last stitch, k1.

Row 2 (WS) and all WS rows: Purl.

Rows 7, 9, and 11 (RS): K1,*k2, yo, k2, k2tog; repeat from * to end.

Repeat rows 1–12 for lace pattern.

Pattern Notes: Working Increases in Lace

At the outside edge of your final lace pattern repeat, place a movable marker. When you are working raglan increases outside this marker, work them in stockinette stitch until you have a complete set of 6 stitches to work an extra repeat. Move your marker to include these extra 6 stitches inside the lace pattern repeat.

YOKE

Collar

With circular needle, cast on 136 (152, 154, 162, 168, 176, 178, 190, 192) stitches; do not join.

Next row (WS): P35 (40, 41, 43, 45, 48, 49, 52, 53), place marker, p14 (14, 14, 16, 16, 16, 16, 18, 18), place marker, p38 (44, 44, 44, 46, 48, 48, 50, 50), place marker, p14 (14, 14, 16, 16, 16, 16, 18, 18), place marker, purl to end of row.

Next row (RS): Work lace pattern repeat 5 (6, 6, 7, 7, 7, 8, 8, 8) times, *knit to marker, slip marker; repeat from * 3 more times, k4 (3, 4, 0, 2, 5, 0, 3, 4), work lace pattern repeat 5 (6, 6, 7, 7, 7, 8, 8, 8) times, k1.

Work in pattern established until work measures 2½" (6.5cm), ending with a wrong-side row.

Short Row Neck Shaping

Row 1 (RS): Work in pattern established to 1 stitch before fourth marker, turn work.

Row 2 (WS): Slip stitch, place safety pin, work to 1 stitch before first marker in row, turn work.

Row 3 (RS): Slip stitch, place safety pin, work to 4 stitches before previous gap, turn work.

Row 4 (WS): Slip stitch, place safety pin, work to 4 stitches before previous gap, turn work.

Repeat rows 3 and 4 three more times.

Work next right-side row to end, working yarn loops together with their corresponding stitch.

Work next wrong-side row to end, working yarn loops together with their corresponding stitch.

Raglan Shoulder Shaping

Incorporate front stitches into lace pattern when you have enough stitches.

Note: For some sizes, the increase stitch will be taken from the edge of the lace panel for the first increase.

Inc Row 1 (RS): *Work in pattern established to last stitch before marker, kfb, slip marker, kfb; repeat from * 3 more times, work to end of row—8 stitches increased.

Next row (WS): Purl.

Repeat these 2 rows 11 (9, 9, 14, 17, 17, 22, 25, 26) more times—232 (232, 234, 282, 312, 320, 362, 398, 408) stitches total; 47 (50, 51, 58, 63, 66, 72, 78, 80) stitches each front, 38 (34, 34, 46, 52, 52, 62, 70, 72) stitches each sleeve, 62 (64, 64, 74, 82, 84, 94, 102, 104) back stitches.

Sizes 30 (32¾)" (76 [83]cm) only: Continue below at **.

SIZES – (–, 36, 38¾, 42, 44¾, 48, 50¾, 54)"
(– [–, 91, 98.5, 106.5, 113.5, 122, 129, 137]CM)

Inc Row 1 (RS): *Work in pattern established to last stitch before marker, kfb, slip marker, kfb; repeat from * 3 more times, work to end of row—8 stitches increased.

Next row (WS): Purl.

Inc Row 2 (RS): Work in pattern established to last stitch before first marker, kfb, slip marker, knit to second marker, slip marker, kfb, knit to last stitch before marker, kfb, slip marker, knit to last marker, slip marker, kfb, work in pattern established to end of row—4 stitches increased.

Next row (WS): Purl.

Repeat these 4 rows – (–, 2, 3, 4, 5, 6, 7, 9) more times for – (–, 270, 330, 372, 392, 446, 494, 528) stitches total; – (–, 57, 66, 73, 78, 86, 94, 100) stitches each front, – (–, 40, 54, 62, 64, 76, 86, 92) stitches each sleeve, – (–, 76, 90, 102, 108, 122, 134, 144) back stitches.

Size 54" (137cm) only: Yoke is complete; continue with Body.

established to end of row—212 (232, 254, 274, 296, 316, 338, 358, 380) stitches total; 90 (98, 108, 116, 126, 134, 144, 152, 162) back stitches, 61 (67, 73, 79, 85, 91, 97, 103, 109) stitches each front.

Next row (WS): Work in lace pattern to side marker, slip marker, work in stockinette stitch across back to next side marker, work in lace pattern to end of row.

Continue in pattern established until body measures 2" (5cm) from underarm, ending with a wrong-side row.

Place removable dart marker 30 (32, 36, 38, 42, 44, 48, 50, 54) stitches inside each side marker on the back.

Waist Dec Row (RS): Work in pattern established to 2 stitches before first dart marker, k2tog, slip marker, work in pattern established to next dart marker, slip marker, ssk, work in pattern established to end of row—2 stitches decreased.

Work waist dec row every 6 rows 9 more times—192 (212, 234, 254, 276, 296, 318, 338, 360) stitches total; 70 (78, 88, 96, 106, 114, 124, 132, 142) back stitches, 61 (67, 73, 79, 85, 91, 97, 103, 109) stitches each front.

Work 11 rows even in pattern established.

Hip Inc Row (RS): Work in pattern established to first dart marker, M1R, slip marker, work in pattern established to next dart marker, slip marker, M1L, work in pattern established to end of row—2 stitches increased.

Work hip inc row every 4 rows 9 more times—212 (232, 254, 274, 296, 316, 338, 358, 380) stitches total; 90 (98, 108, 116, 126, 134, 144, 152, 162) back stitches, 61 (67, 73, 79, 85, 91, 97, 103, 109) stitches each front.

Work even in pattern until body measures 14" (35.5cm) from underarm or desired length. Bind off all stitches using elastic bind-off.

SLEEVES

Sleeves are worked with long circular needle using Magic Loop method; substitute double-pointed needles if you prefer.

SIZES 30 (32¾, 36, 38¾, 42, 44¾, 48, 50¾, –)" (76 [83, 91.5, 98.5, 106.5, 113.5, 122, 129, –]CM)

**Inc Row 1 (RS): *Work in pattern established to last stitch before marker, kfb, slip marker, kfb; repeat from * 3 more times, work in pattern established to end of row—8 stitches increased.

Work 3 rows even in pattern.

Repeat these 4 rows 10 (12, 10, 7, 5, 5, 2, 0, –) more times—320 (336, 358, 394, 420, 440, 470, 502, –) stitches total; 58 (63, 68, 74, 79, 84, 89, 95, –) stitches each front, 60 (60, 62, 70, 74, 76, 82, 88, –) stitches each sleeve, 84 (90, 98, 106, 114, 120, 128, 136, –) back stitches.

BODY

Sleeve Divide Row (RS): *Work in pattern established to marker, remove marker, slip 60 (60, 62, 70, 74, 76, 82, 88, 92) sleeve stitches onto waste yarn, remove marker, using backward-loop method, cast on 3 (4, 5, 5, 6, 7, 8, 8, 9) stitches, place marker for side seam, cast on 3 (4, 5, 5, 6, 7, 8, 8, 9) stitches; repeat from * once, work in pattern

Starting at center of underarm cast-on stitches, with circular needle (or double-pointed needles), pick up and knit 3 (4, 5, 5, 6, 7, 8, 8, 9) stitches, place 60 (60, 62, 70, 74, 76, 82, 88, 92) stitches from waste yarn onto needle, knit these stitches, pick up and knit remaining 3 (4, 5, 5, 6, 7, 8, 8, 9) stitches from underarm stitches, place marker for start of round—66 (68, 72, 80, 86, 90, 98, 104, 110) stitches.

Knit 26 (26, 26, 14, 13, 11, 9, 8, 7) rounds even.

Sleeve Dec Rnd: K1, k2tog, knit to last 3 stitches, ssk, k1—64 (66, 70, 78, 84, 88, 96, 102, 108); 2 stitches decreased.

Work these 27 (27, 27, 15, 14, 12, 10, 9, 8) rounds 2 (2, 2, 5, 6, 7, 9, 11, 12) more times—60 (62, 66, 68, 72, 74, 78, 80, 84) stitches.

Work even until sleeve measures 11½ (11½, 12, 12, 12½, 12½, 13, 13, 13)" (29 [29, 30.5, 30.5, 32, 32, 33, 33, 33]cm) from underarm or desired length. Bind off all stitches using elastic bind-off.

Repeat for second sleeve.

FINISHING

Using tapestry needle, weave in all loose ends. Gently block to dimensions given on schematic, taking care to open up lace fabric. Allow to gently roll at edges.

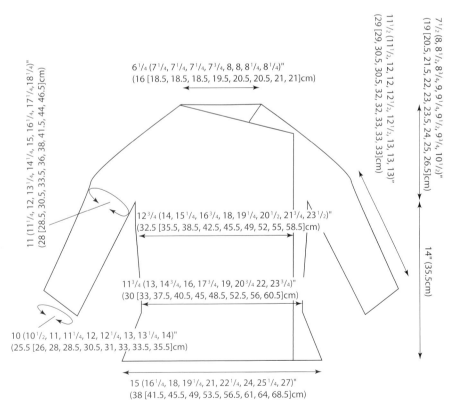

6¼ (7¼, 7¼, 7¼, 7¾, 8, 8, 8¼, 8¼)"
(16 [18.5, 18.5, 18.5, 19.5, 20.5, 20.5, 21, 21]cm)

11 (11¼, 12, 13¼, 14¼, 15, 16¼, 17¼, 18¼)"
(28 [28.5, 30.5, 33.5, 36, 38, 41.5, 44, 46.5]cm)

12¾ (14, 15¼, 16¾, 18, 19¼, 20½, 21¾, 23½)"
(32.5 [35.5, 38.5, 42.5, 45.5, 49, 52, 55, 58.5]cm)

11¾ (13, 14¾, 16, 17¾, 19, 20¾ 22, 23¾)"
(30 [33, 37.5, 40.5, 45, 48.5, 52.5, 56, 60.5]cm)

10 (10½, 11, 11¼, 12, 12¼, 13, 13¼, 14)"
(25.5 [26, 28, 28.5, 30.5, 31, 33, 33.5, 35.5]cm)

15 (16¼, 18, 19¼, 21, 22¼, 24, 25¼, 27)"
(38 [41.5, 45.5, 49, 53.5, 56.5, 61, 64, 68.5]cm)

11½ (11½, 12, 12, 12½, 12½, 13, 13, 13)"
(29 [29, 30.5, 30.5, 32, 32, 33, 33, 33]cm)

7½ (8, 8½, 8¾, 9, 9¼, 9½, 9¾, 10½)"
(19 [20.5, 21.5, 22, 23, 23.5, 24, 25, 26.5]cm)

14" (35.5cm)

Note: Collar is not shown in schematic.

lagarto

DOLMAN PULLOVER

Worked from the bottom up, this easy-to-wear sweater creates unique wavelike patterns using a striped yarn and drop-stitch short row sections at the hips. The sleeves and shoulders are shaped entirely using short rows. Wear this sweater with plenty of positive ease for an oversized, relaxed feel. To downplay the drop-stitch hip panel, use a solid or semisolid yarn instead of the self-striping yarn.

Skill Level Intermediate

Sizes and Finished Measurements

To Fit Bust Circumference (up to)	30" (76cm)	32¾" (83cm)	36½" (92.5cm)	39¼" (99.5cm)	42" (106.5cm)	46" (117cm)	48¾" (124cm)	52½" (133.5cm)	55¼" (140.5cm)
Bust Size	34" (86cm)	36¾" (93.5cm)	40½" (103cm)	43¼" (110cm)	46" (117cm)	50" (127cm)	52¾" (134cm)	56½" (143.5cm)	59¼" (150.5cm)
Length	24½" (62cm)	25½" (64.5cm)	26¼" (67cm)	27" (68.5cm)	27¾" (70.5cm)	28¼" (72cm)	29¼" (74.5cm)	29¾" (75.5cm)	30¼" (77cm)

Size 40½" (103cm) modeled with 6" (15cm) of positive ease

Materials

YARN

6 (7, 8, 8, 9, 10, 10, 11, 12) skeins Noro Kirara, 51% wool, 29% cotton, 10% silk, 10% angora, 1.76 oz (50g), 164 yd (150m), in color 10 **3** light

NEEDLES & NOTIONS

1 US size 7 (4.5mm) circular needle, 32" (81cm) long (or longer for larger sizes)

1 US size 7 (4.5mm) circular needle, 40" (101.5cm) long

Adjust needle size as necessary to achieve gauge.

Lockable stitch markers

Stitch holders or waste yarn

(continues)

NEEDLES & NOTIONS (continued)

US size 7 (4.5mm) crochet hook

Tapestry needle

Gauge

17 stitches and 28 rows = 4" (10cm) in stockinette stitch, blocked

17 stitches and 36 rows = 4" (10cm) in garter stitch, blocked

Short Row Method Used

Wrap and Turn (page 10)

Techniques

For other techniques used in the pattern, please refer to General Techniques (page 155).

SINGLE CROCHET

Begin with slip knot on your crochet hook.

*Insert hook into stitch on your knitting, yarn over hook, pull loop through your knitting, yarn over hook again and pull this second loop through both loops on your hook; repeat from * until you have completed your edging.

Pattern Notes

• When working short rows at the hem, use a lockable stitch marker to mark the position of the turn. This marker can then be moved every time you make a new short row.

• When working the short rows at the hem, wrap-and-turn short rows are worked but the wraps are not picked up; the dropped-stitch pattern hides them well.

• For the sleeves and shoulders, the wraps are picked up and worked with the stitch they wrap, as this is a very visible location.

BODY

With shorter circular needle, cast on 144 (156, 172, 184, 196, 212, 224, 240, 252) stitches, place a marker for the start of the round, and join to work in the round. Place marker for side seam at halfway point.

Rnd 1: Knit.

Rnd 2: Purl.

Repeat these 2 rounds of garter stitch 5 more times.

Drop-Stitch Wedge

*Setup Row 1: K36 (39, 43, 46, 49, 53, 56, 60, 63) past marker, w&t.

Setup Row 2: K72 (78, 86, 92, 98, 106, 112, 120, 126), w&t.

Row 1 (RS): Knit to 3 stitches before previous wrap, w&t.

Row 2 (WS): Knit to 3 stitches before previous wrap, w&t.

Double-Stitch Row (RS): Knit to 3 stitches before previous wrap, wrapping yarn around right needle twice before pulling needle through stitch, w&t.

Drop-Stitch Row (WS): Knit to 3 stitches before previous wrap, dropping extra yarn loop from needle as you knit, w&t.

Repeat these last 4 rows 4 (4, 5, 5, 6, 6, 6, 7, 7) more times.

Knit to end of round.*

Work 8 rounds in garter stitch, ending with a purl round.

Knit to side seam and work from * to * as before. (Note that this set of short rows is on the other side of the garment).

Stockinette Stitch Short Rows

*Setup Row 1 (RS): K39 (42, 47, 53, 56, 61, 66, 72, 75), w&t.

Setup Row 2 (WS): P6 (6, 8, 14, 14, 16, 20, 24, 24), w&t.

Row 1 (RS): Knit to previously wrapped stitch, knit wrap with stitch it wraps, k2, w&t.

Row 2 (WS): Purl to previously wrapped stitch, purl wrap with stitch it wraps, p2, w&t.

Repeat these 2 rows 9 (10, 11, 11, 12, 13, 13, 14, 15) more times.*

Knit to side marker.

Work Stockinette Stitch Short Rows from * to * once more. (Note that this set of short rows is on the other side of the garment.)

Work even in stockinette stitch until body measures 13¾" (35cm) from cast-on edge.

YOKE BACK
Sleeve Gusset
Inc Row (RS): With longer circular needle, k2, M1L, knit to 2 stitches before side marker, M1R, k2. This will be the back of the sweater; the remainder of the stitches will stay on the original circular needle to be worked later—72 (78, 86, 92, 98, 106, 112, 120, 126) stitches held, 74 (80, 88, 94, 100, 108, 114, 122, 128) stitches on working needle.

Next row (WS): Purl all stitches.

Repeat these 2 rows 3 (3, 4, 4, 5, 5, 6, 6, 7) more times—80 (86, 96, 102, 110, 118, 126, 134, 142) stitches.

Sleeves
***Sleeve Cast-On Row 1 (RS):** Using cable cast-on method, cast on 52 (52, 53, 53, 54, 54, 55, 57, 58) stitches, knit to end of row.

Sleeve Cast-On Row 2 (WS): Using cable cast-on method, cast on 52 (52, 53, 53, 54, 54, 55, 57, 58) stitches, k9, purl to last 9 stitches, k6, slip 3 stitches purlwise with yarn in front—184 (190, 202, 208, 218, 226, 236, 248, 258) stitches.

Row 1 (RS): Knit to last 3 stitches, slip 3 stitches purlwise with yarn in front.

Row 2 (WS): K9, purl to last 9 stitches, k6, slip 3 stitches purlwise with yarn in front.

Work these last 2 rows 20 (22, 23, 24, 25, 26, 27, 28, 28) more times.

Sleeve Shaping
Short Row 1 (RS): Work in pattern to last 15 (15, 16, 16, 16, 16, 16, 16, 17) stitches, w&t.

Short Row 2 (WS): Purl to last 15 (15, 16, 16, 16, 16, 16, 16, 17) stitches, w&t.

Short Row 3 (RS): Knit to 6 (6, 7, 7, 7, 7, 7, 7, 8) stitches before previously wrapped stitch, w&t.

Short Row 4 (WS): Purl to 6 (6, 7, 7, 7, 7, 7, 7, 8) stitches before previously wrapped stitch, w&t.

Work short rows 3 and 4 four more times.*

Shoulder Shaping
Place stitch marker at each side of the central 32 (32, 34, 36, 36, 38, 38, 40, 40) stitches. This marks the position of the neck.

Short Row 1 (RS): Knit to 19 (22, 25, 27, 30, 33, 36, 39, 42) stitches past second neck marker, w&t.

Short Row 2 (WS): Purl to 19 (22, 25, 27, 30, 33, 36, 39, 42) stitches past second neck marker, w&t.

Short Row 3 (RS): Knit to 3 stitches before previously wrapped stitch, w&t.

Short Row 4 (WS): Purl to 3 stitches before previously wrapped stitch, w&t.

Work short rows 3 and 4 as above 2 (3, 4, 5, 6, 7, 8, 9, 10) more times.

Each side of the back is now worked separately with 2 balls of yarn. Instructions for each side are divided by a semicolon.

Neck Bind-Off Row (RS): Knit to first neck marker, remove marker, ssk, k2 and drop yarn, with second ball of yarn, bind off 24 (24, 26, 28, 28, 30, 30, 32, 32) stitches, k2, k2tog, remove marker, knit to 3 stitches before previously wrapped stitch, w&t.

Neck Dec Row (WS): Purl to 4 stitches before neck, p2tog, p2; p2, ssp, purl to 3 stitches before previously wrapped stitch, w&t.

Neck Dec Row (RS): Knit to 4 stitches before neck, ssk, k2; k2, k2tog, knit to 3 stitches before previously wrapped stitch, w&t.

Work 1 more wrong-side Neck Dec Row.

Work in pattern to end of right-side row, picking up all wraps and working them with the stitch they wrap.

Work 1 more wrong-side row, picking up all wraps and working them with the stitch they wrap.

Set aside stitches to be worked later—76 (79, 84, 86, 91, 94, 99, 104, 109) stitches each side.

YOKE FRONT

Sleeve Gusset
Inc Row (RS): Rejoin yarn to right side of held stitches, with longer circular needle, k2, M1L, knit to 2 stitches before side marker, M1R, k2—74 (80, 88, 94, 100, 108, 114, 122, 128) stitches.

Next row (WS): Purl all stitches.

Repeat these 2 rows 3 (3, 4, 4, 5, 5, 6, 6, 7) more times—80 (86, 96, 102, 110, 118, 126, 134, 142) stitches.

Work Sleeves as for Back from * to *.

Shoulder and Neck Shaping
Each side of the front is now worked separately with different balls of yarn. Instructions for each side are divided by a semicolon.

Place stitch marker at each side of the central 16 (16, 16, 16, 16, 18, 18, 18, 18) stitches. This marks the position of the neck. Place markers at each side of central 72 (78, 86, 92, 98, 106, 112, 120, 126) stitches to mark position of shoulders.

Neck Bind-Off Row (RS): Knit to first neck marker, drop yarn, remove marker, with second ball of yarn, bind off 16 (16, 16, 16, 16, 18, 18, 18, 18) stitches, remove marker, knit to 1 stitch before shoulder marker, w&t.

Neck Dec Row (WS): Purl to 4 stitches before neck, p2tog, p2; p2, ssp, purl to 1 stitch before shoulder marker, w&t.

Neck Dec Row (RS): Knit to 4 stitches before neck, ssk, k2; k2, k2tog, knit to 3 stitches before previously wrapped stitch, w&t.

Neck Dec Row (WS): Purl to 4 stitches before neck, p2tog, p2; p2, ssp, purl to 3 stitches before previously wrapped stitch, w&t.

Work these last 2 neck dec rows once more.

Work right-side neck dec row.

Next row (WS): Purl right side; purl to 3 stitches before previously wrapped stitch, w&t.

Work these last 2 rows 2 (2, 3, 4, 4, 4, 4, 5, 5) more times—76 (79, 84, 86, 91, 94, 99, 104, 109) stitches each side.

Short rows for size 34" (86.5cm) are now complete; proceed to All Sizes.

SIZES: – (36¾, 40½, 43¼, 46, 50, 52¾, 56½, 59¼)" (– [93.5, 103, 110, 117, 127, 134, 143.5, 150.5]CM)

Short Row 1 (RS): Knit left side; knit to 3 stitches before previously wrapped stitch, w&t.

Short Row 2 (WS): Purl right side; purl to 3 stitches before previously wrapped stitch, w&t.

Work Short Rows 1 and 2 as above – (0, 0, 0, 1, 2, 3, 3, 4) more times.

ALL SIZES

Work in pattern to end of right-side row, picking up all wraps and working them with the stitch they wrap.

Work 1 more wrong-side row, picking up all wraps and working them with the stitch they wrap.

Turn garment inside out so the right side of front and back are facing each other. Using three-needle bind-off, join the 76 (79, 84, 86, 91, 94, 99, 104, 109) stitches from front and back of each shoulder together.

FINISHING

Seam bottom of sleeves and sleeve gussets together.

Starting at the center of the back neck, work single crochet around the neck opening.

Weave in all loose ends. Block garment to dimensions given on schematic.

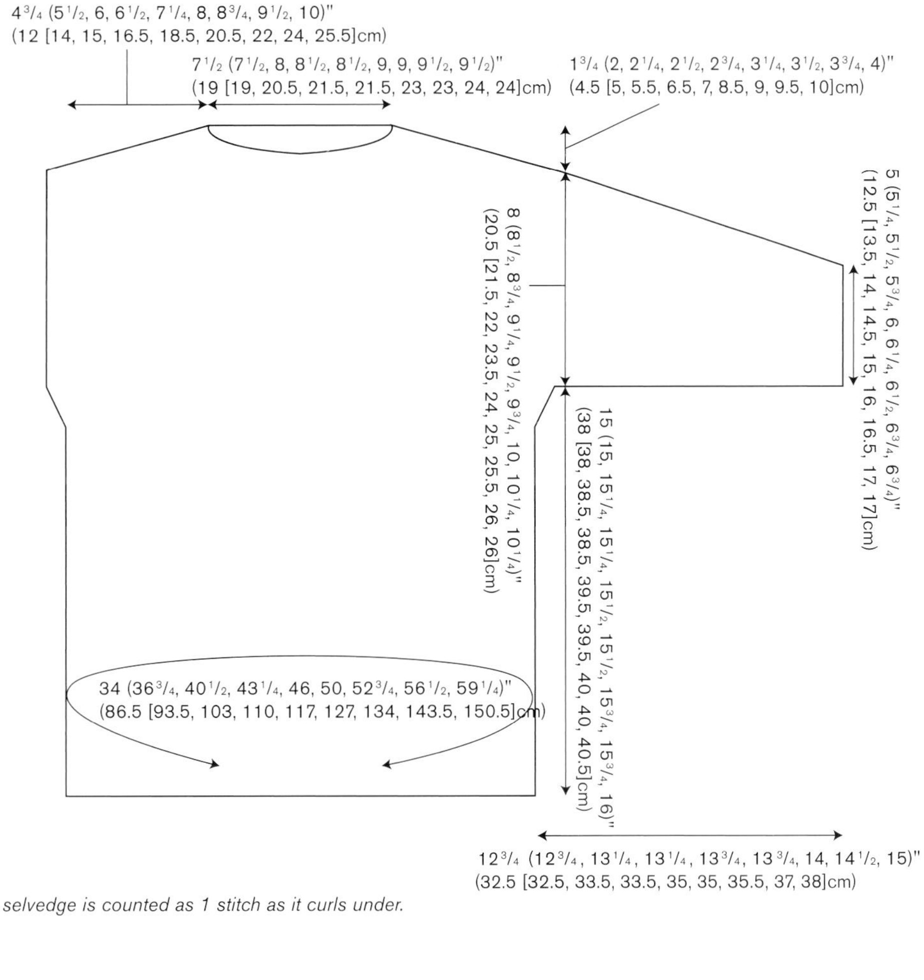

4¾ (5½, 6, 6½, 7¼, 8, 8¾, 9½, 10)"
(12 [14, 15, 16.5, 18.5, 20.5, 22, 24, 25.5]cm)
7½ (7½, 8, 8½, 8½, 9, 9, 9½, 9½)"
(19 [19, 20.5, 21.5, 21.5, 23, 23, 24, 24]cm)
1¾ (2, 2¼, 2½, 2¾, 3¼, 3½, 3¾, 4)"
(4.5 [5, 5.5, 6.5, 7, 8.5, 9, 9.5, 10]cm)
5 (5¼, 5½, 5¾, 6, 6¼, 6½, 6¾, 6¾)"
(12.5 [13.5, 14, 14.5, 15, 16, 16.5, 17, 17]cm)
8 (8½, 8¾, 9¼, 9½, 9¾, 10, 10¼, 10¼)"
(20.5 [21.5, 22, 23.5, 24, 25, 25.5, 26, 26]cm)
15 (15, 15¼, 15¼, 15½, 15½, 15¾, 15¾, 16)"
(38 [38, 38.5, 38.5, 39.5, 39.5, 40, 40, 40.5]cm)
34 (36¾, 40½, 43¼, 46, 50, 52¾, 56½, 59¼)"
(86.5 [93.5, 103, 110, 117, 127, 134, 143.5, 150.5]cm)
12¾ (12¾, 13¼, 13¼, 13¾, 13¾, 14, 14½, 15)"
(32.5 [32.5, 33.5, 33.5, 35, 35, 35.5, 37, 38]cm)

Note: I-cord sleeve selvedge is counted as 1 stitch as it curls under.

riyito
OVERSIZED SWEATER

The lovely drape in this sweater and the curved hem create a flattering top with a relaxed fit. The back and front are knit separately from the top down to the underarm using short rows to smoothly create the shoulder slope. The body is then knit in one piece to the bottom, where short rows are again used to create the hem curve across the back.

Skill Level Intermediate

Sizes and Finished Measurements

To Fit Bust Circumference (up to)	30" (76cm)	34" (86cm)	37" (94cm)	41" (104cm)	43" (109cm)	47" (119.5cm)	49" (124.5cm)	52" (132cm)	55" (140cm)
Bust Size	39¼" (99.5cm)	43¼" (110cm)	46" (117cm)	50" (127cm)	52" (132cm)	56" (142cm)	58" (147.5cm)	61¼" (155.5cm)	64" (163cm)
Length	28½" (72cm)	29¼" (74.5cm)	30" (76cm)	31¼" (79.5cm)	32" (81cm)	33½" (85cm)	34¼" (87cm)	35¼" (89.5cm)	36¼" (92cm)

Size 46" (117cm) modeled with 11" (28cm) of positive ease

Materials

YARN

5 (6, 6, 7, 7, 8, 9, 9, 10) skeins Manos del Uruguay Silk Blend Fino, 70% wool, 30% silk, 1.76 oz (50g), 246 yds (225m), in color 2220 **(1)** super fine
Note: This yarn is sometimes sold in 3.53 oz (100g) skeins, in which case you need about half the number of skeins.

NEEDLES & NOTIONS

US size 5 (3.75mm) circular needle, 40" (101.5cm) long (or longer for larger sweater size)
US size 5 (3.75mm) circular needle, 32" (81cm) long
1 set US size 5 (3.75mm) double-pointed needles
Adjust needle size as necessary to achieve gauge.
Safety pins for Japanese short rows
Stitch holders or waste yarn

(continues)

Stitch markers

Tapestry needle

Gauge

24 stitches and 35 rows = 4" (10cm) in stockinette stitch, blocked

24 stitches and 40 rows = 4" (10cm) in texture stitch, blocked

24 stitches and 44 rows = 4" (10cm) in garter stitch, blocked

Short Row Methods Used

Japanese (page 14) and German (page 18)

Techniques

For other techniques used in the pattern, please refer to General Techniques (page 155).

TEXTURE STITCH (WORKED FLAT; MULTIPLE OF 2 STITCHES PLUS 1)

Row 1 (RS): Knit.

Rows 2 and 4 (WS): Purl.

Row 3 (RS): *K1, p1; repeat from * to last stitch, k1.

Repeat rows 1–4 for texture stitch pattern.

TEXTURE STITCH (WORKED IN THE ROUND; MULTIPLE OF 2 STITCHES)

Rnds 1, 2, and 4: Knit.

Rnd 3: *K1, p1; repeat from * to end of round.

Repeat rounds 1–4 for texture stitch pattern.

GARTER STITCH

Rnd 1: Knit.

Rnd 2: Purl.

Repeat rounds 1–2 for garter stitch.

Pattern Notes

- The shoulder slope is created using Japanese short rows. When you pass each yarn loop, ensure that you work it with the corresponding stitch.

- Short rows at the hem are created using German short rows. Ensure every double stitch is worked as a single stitch.

BACK

Right Back Shoulder

With shorter circular needle, cast on 38 (44, 46, 52, 54, 60, 62, 66, 70) stitches.

Work 4 rows in garter stitch.

Short Row 1 (RS): K3, turn work.

Next row (WS): Slip stitch, place safety pin, purl to end.

Short Row 2 (RS): K6 (*working yarn loop with stitch as you pass*), turn work.

Next row (WS): Slip stitch, place safety pin, purl to end.

Short Row 3 (RS): K1, M1R, k8, turn work.

Next row (WS): Slip stitch, place safety pin, purl to last stitch, M1P, p1.

Short Row 4 (RS): K1, M1R, k13, turn work.

Next row (WS): Slip stitch, place safety pin, purl to last stitch, M1P, p1—42 (48, 50, 56, 58, 64, 66, 70, 74) stitches.

Break yarn and set the stitches aside on a holder.

Left Back Shoulder

With shorter circular needle, cast on 38 (44, 46, 52, 54, 60, 62, 66, 70) stitches.

Work 5 rows in garter stitch.

Short Row 1 (WS): P3, turn work.

Next row (RS): Slip stitch, place safety pin, knit to end.

Short Row 2 (WS): P6, turn work.

Next row (RS): Slip stitch, place safety pin, knit to last stitch, M1L, k1.

Short Row 3 (WS): P1, M1P, p9, turn work.

Next row (RS): Slip stitch, place safety pin, knit to last stitch, M1L, k1.

Short Row 4 (WS): P1, M1P, p14, turn work—42 (48, 50, 56, 58, 64, 66, 70, 74) stitches.

Complete Back

Joining Row (RS): Slip stitch, place safety pin, knit left back shoulder stitches, cast on 35 (35, 39, 39, 41, 41, 43, 45, 45) stitches using backward-loop cast-on, knit right back shoulder stitches to 3 stitches past previous gap, turn work—119 (131, 139, 151, 157, 169, 175, 185, 193) stitches.

Next row (WS): Slip stitch, place safety pin, purl to 3 stitches past previous gap, turn work.

Next row (RS): Slip stitch, place safety pin, knit to 3 stitches past previous gap, turn work.

Work these 2 rows 6 (7, 8, 10, 11, 13, 13, 15, 16) more times.

Work 1 more wrong-side row.

Next row (RS): Slip stitch, place safety pin, knit to the end of the row, working final yarn loop together with the stitch as you pass it.

Work 3 rows in garter stitch.

Work even in texture stitch until work at the armhole edge measures 5¾ (6, 6¼, 6½, 6¾, 7¼, 7¾, 8¼, 8¾)" (14.5 [15, 16, 16.5, 17, 18.5, 19.5, 21, 22]cm), ending with a wrong-side row.

Set stitches aside and break yarn.

FRONT

Left Front Shoulder

With longer circular needle and right side of work facing, pick up and knit 38 (44, 46, 52, 54, 60, 62, 66, 70) stitches from left back shoulder cast-on stitches. Work 3 rows in garter stitch.

Short Row 1 (RS): K3, turn work.

Next row (WS): Slip stitch, place safety pin, purl to end.

Short Row 2 (RS): Knit to 3 stitches past previous gap (*working yarn loop with correct stitch as you pass it*), turn work.

Next row (WS): Slip stitch, place safety pin, purl to end.

Work these last 2 rows 0 (1, 0, 2, 3, 5, 4, 6, 7) more times.

Neck Inc Row 1 (RS): K2, M1L, knit to 3 stitches past previous gap, turn work—1 stitch increased.

Next row (WS): Slip stitch, place safety pin, purl to end.

Work these last 2 rows 5 (5, 7, 7, 7, 7, 8, 7, 7) more times—44 (50, 54, 60, 62, 68, 71, 74, 78) stitches.

Work neck inc row 1.

Neck Inc Row 2 (WS): Slip stitch, place safety pin, purl to last 2 stitches, M1P, p2—1 stitch increased.

Work these 2 rows 3 (3, 3, 3, 3, 3, 3, 4, 4) more times—52 (58, 62, 68, 70, 76, 79, 84, 88) stitches.

Set stitches aside on holder and break yarn.

Right Front Shoulder

With longer circular needle and right side of work facing, pick up and knit 38 (44, 46, 52, 54, 60, 62, 66, 70) stitches from right back shoulder cast-on stitches.

Work 4 rows in garter stitch.

Short Row 1 (WS): P3, turn work.

Next row (RS): Slip stitch, place safety pin, knit to end.

Short Row 2 (WS): Purl to 3 stitches past previous gap (*working yarn loop with stitch as you pass it*), turn work.

Next row (RS): Slip stitch, place safety pin, knit.

Work these last 2 rows 0 (1, 0, 2, 3, 5, 4, 6, 7) more times.

Next row (WS): Purl to 3 stitches past previous gap, turn work.

Neck Inc Row 1 (RS): Slip stitch, place safety pin, knit to last 2 stitches, M1R, k2—1 stitch increased.

Next row (WS): Purl to 3 stitches past previous gap, turn work.

Work these last 2 rows 5 (5, 7, 7, 7, 7, 8, 7, 7) more times—44 (50, 54, 60, 62, 68, 71, 74, 78) stitches.

Work neck inc row 1.

Neck Inc Row 2 (WS): P2, M1P, purl to 3 stitches past previous gap, turn work—1 stitch increased.

Work these 2 rows 3 (3, 3, 3, 3, 3, 3, 4, 4) more times— 52 (58, 62, 68, 70, 76, 79, 84, 88) stitches.

Neck Cast-On Row (RS): Slip stitch, place safety pin, knit to end of right front shoulder stitches, using backward-loop method, cast on 15 (15, 15, 15, 17, 17, 17, 17, 17) stitches, work all left front shoulder stitches—119 (131, 139, 151, 157, 169, 175, 185, 193) stitches.

Work 3 rows even in garter stitch.

Work even in texture stitch until work at the armhole edge measures 5¾ (6, 6¼, 6½, 6¾, 7¼, 7¾, 8¼, 8¾)" (14.5

[15, 16, 16.5, 17, 18.5, 19.5, 21, 22]cm), ensuring you end on the same wrong-side texture stitch row as on the back.

BODY

Work front stitches in pattern to the last stitch, k2tog (one from front and one from back), work back stitches in pattern to the last stitch, place marker for start of round, k2tog (one from back and one from front)—236 (260, 276, 300, 312, 336, 348, 368, 384) stitches.

Continue to work the body even in texture stitch pattern in the round until it measures 11¼ (11½, 11¾, 12, 12¼, 12¼, 12¼, 12¼, 12¼)" (28.5 [29, 30, 30.5, 31, 31, 31, 31, 31]cm) from where it was joined.

Hem

Short rows for hem are worked using German short rows.

Work even in garter stitch for 4 rounds.

Work even in stockinette stitch for 14 rounds.

Short Row 1 (RS): K29 (32, 34, 37, 39, 42, 43, 46, 48), turn work.

Short Row 2 (WS): Slip stitch purlwise with yarn in front, pull yarn over needle so that 2 strands are visible at top of needle, p175 (193, 205, 223, 233, 251, 259, 275, 287), turn work.

Short Row 3 (RS): Slip stitch as before, knit to 3 stitches before previous double stitch, turn work.

Short Row 4 (WS): Slip stitch as before, place marker, purl to 3 stitches before previous double stitch, turn work.

Work short rows 3 and 4 as above 6 (7, 7, 8, 8, 9, 9, 10, 11) more times.

Short Row 5 (RS): Slip stitch as before, knit to 2 stitches before previous double stitch, turn work.

Short Row 6 (WS): Slip stitch as before, purl to 2 stitches before previous double stitch, turn work.

Work short rows 5 and 6 as above 7 (7, 7, 7, 7, 8, 9, 9, 9) more times.

Short Row 7 (RS): Slip stitch as before, knit to 1 stitch before previous double stitch, turn work.

Short Row 8 (WS): Slip stitch as before, purl to 1 stitch before previous double stitch, turn work.

Work short rows 7 and 8 as above 7 more times.

Knit to the end of the round, working every double stitch as a single stitch.

Work even in garter stitch for 12 rounds, taking care on first complete round to work every double stitch as a single stitch.

Bind off all stitches using an I-cord bind-off.

SLEEVES

Using double-pointed needles and starting at the center of the underarm, pick up and knit 35 (36, 38, 39, 41, 43, 47, 50, 53) stitches evenly to the top of the shoulder, pick up and knit 35 (36, 38, 39, 41, 43, 47, 50, 53) stitches evenly to the center of the underarm—70 (72, 76, 78, 82, 86, 94, 100, 106) stitches.

Work even in stockinette stitch for 17 rounds.

Sleeve Dec Rnd: K2tog, work to last 2 stitches, ssk—2 stitches decreased.

Work sleeve dec rnd every 7 (7, 7, 6, 6, 5, 4, 4, 4) rounds 7 (8, 9, 10, 12, 14, 17, 19, 20) more times—54 (54, 56, 56, 56, 56, 58, 60, 64) stitches.

Work even in stockinette stitch until sleeve measures 9 (9½, 10, 10, 10½, 11, 11, 11½, 11½)" (23 [24, 25.5, 25.5, 26.5, 28, 28, 29, 29]cm) from armhole or desired length.

Work for 1" (2.5cm) in garter stitch.

Bind off all stitches using an I-cord bind-off.

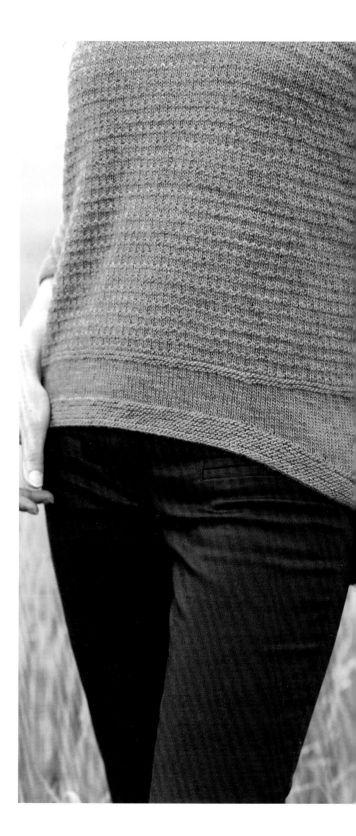

FINISHING

With the circular needle, starting at the right side of the back of neck, pick up stitches around the neck opening.

Bind off all neck stitches using an I-cord bind-off.

Weave in all loose ends. Block garment to dimensions on schematic.

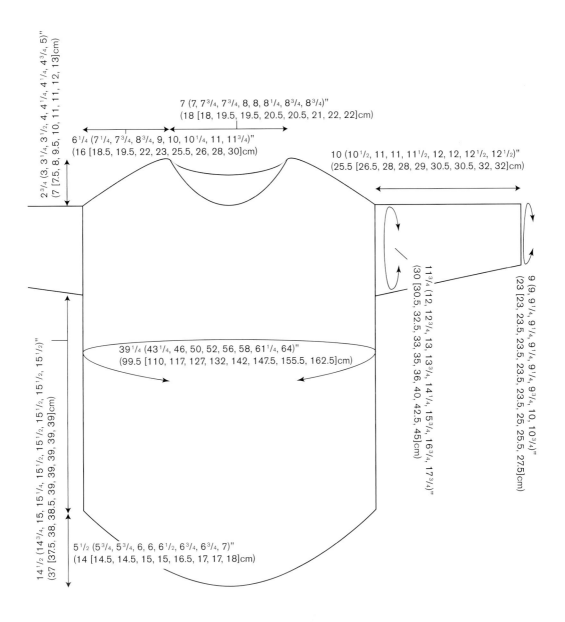

2³/₄ (3, 3¹/₄, 3¹/₂, 4, 4¹/₄, 4¹/₄, 4³/₄, 5)" (7 [7.5, 8, 8.5, 10, 11, 11, 12, 13]cm)

7 (7, 7³/₄, 7³/₄, 8, 8, 8¹/₄, 8³/₄, 8³/₄)" (18 [18, 19.5, 19.5, 20.5, 20.5, 21, 22, 22]cm)

6¹/₄ (7¹/₄, 7³/₄, 8³/₄, 9, 10, 10¹/₄, 11, 11³/₄)" (16 [18.5, 19.5, 22, 23, 25.5, 26, 28, 30]cm)

10 (10¹/₂, 11, 11, 11¹/₂, 12, 12, 12¹/₂, 12¹/₂)" (25.5 [26.5, 28, 28, 29, 30.5, 30.5, 32, 32]cm)

11³/₄ (12, 12³/₄, 13, 13³/₄, 14¹/₄, 15³/₄, 16³/₄, 17³/₄)" (30 [30.5, 32.5, 33, 35, 36, 40, 42.5, 45]cm)

9 (9, 9¹/₄, 9¹/₄, 9¹/₄, 9³/₄, 10, 10³/₄)" (23 [23, 23.5, 23.5, 23.5, 25, 25.5, 27.5]cm)

39¹/₄ (43¹/₄, 46, 50, 52, 56, 58, 61¹/₄, 64)" (99.5 [110, 117, 127, 132, 142, 147.5, 155.5, 162.5]cm)

14¹/₂ (14³/₄, 15, 15¹/₄, 15¹/₂, 15¹/₂, 15¹/₂, 15¹/₂, 15¹/₂)" (37 [37.5, 38, 38.5, 39, 39, 39, 39, 39]cm)

5¹/₂ (5³/₄, 5³/₄, 6, 6, 6¹/₂, 6³/₄, 6³/₄, 7)" (14 [14.5, 14.5, 15, 15, 16.5, 17, 17, 18]cm)

jimenez SIDE-TO-SIDE LINEN TOP

Linen yarn creates unique knitted garments that look diaphanous when knitted loosely, enhanced by exposed seams and dropped stitches. The natural stretch of linen works to your advantage in creating the flattering drape of this sweater, which is started at the center back and worked from side to side

Skill Level Intermediate

Sizes and Finished Measurements

To Fit Bust Circumference (up to)	29" (74cm)	32" (81cm)	35" (89cm)	38" (96.5cm)	41" (104cm)	44" (112cm)	47" (119.5cm)	50" (127cm)	53" (134.5cm)
Bust Size	30" (76cm)	33" (84cm)	36" (91cm)	39" (99cm)	42" (106.5cm)	45" (114cm)	48" (122cm)	51" (129.5cm)	54" (137cm)
Length	21½" (55cm)	22¼" (56.5cm)	22½" (57cm)	23" (58.5cm)	23½" (59.5cm)	23¾" (60cm)	24" (61cm)	24¼" (61.5cm)	24¼" (61.5cm)

Size 36" (91cm) modeled with 1½" (3.8cm) of positive ease

Materials

YARN

4 (4, 4, 5, 5, 6, 6, 6, 6) skeins Shibui Linen, 100% linen, 1.76 oz (50g), 246 yd (225m), in Brick (115) **(2)** fine

NEEDLES & NOTIONS

1 US size 6 (4mm) circular needle, 40" (101.5cm) long

1 US size 6 (4mm) circular needle, 24" (61cm) long

1 set US size 6 (4mm) double-pointed needles (if Magic Loop not used for sleeves)

Adjust needle size as necessary to achieve gauge.

Stitch holders or waste yarn

Stitch markers

Tapestry needle

Gauge

22 stitches and 32 rows = 4" (10cm) in stockinette stitch, blocked

Dropped stitch measures ½" (13mm) deep

Short Row Method Used

Wrap and Turn (page 10)

Techniques

For other techniques used in the pattern, please refer to General Techniques (page 155).

Pattern Notes

- This sweater is knit sideways from the center out. Begin with the right back, join it to the front, and then work one piece all the way to the side. When the right side is complete, stitches are picked up for the left side, which is worked in the same way.
- When M1 is used on the wrong side of reverse stockinette stitch you can choose to use either M1R or M1L, as the directional slope isn't visible on the right side.
- The seam created where the stitches are picked up is deliberately placed on the right side of the work to create an exposed seam.

RIGHT SIDE

Right Back

With longer circular needle and knitted cast-on method, cast on 114 (118, 120, 122, 124, 126, 128, 130, 130) stitches.

Next row (RS): Knit.

Next row (WS): Purl.

*Short Row 1 (RS): K74, w&t.

Next row (WS): Purl to end of row.

Short Row 2 (RS): Knit to 14 stitches before previously wrapped stitch, w&t.

Next row (WS): Purl to end of row.

Repeat these last 2 rows 3 more times.

Next row (RS): Knit to end of row, working all wrapped stitches with the stitch they wrap.

Next row (WS): Purl.*

We are now switching to reverse stockinette stitch.

Next row (RS): Purl.

Next row (WS): Knit.

Work 14 (14, 16, 18, 20, 22, 22, 22, 22) more rows in reverse stockinette stitch.

Neck Inc Row (RS): Purl to last stitch, M1P, p1.

Neck Inc Row (WS): K1, M1, knit to end of row.

Repeat these 2 rows once more—118 (122, 124, 126, 128, 130, 132, 134, 134) stitches.

Set stitches aside but do not break yarn.

Right Front
Using new ball of yarn, with shorter circular needle and knitted cast-on method, cast on 108 (112, 113, 114, 115, 116, 118, 120, 120) stitches.

***Next row (RS):** Knit.

Short Row 1 (WS): P74, w&t.

Next row (RS): Knit to end of row.

Short Row 2 (WS): Purl to 14 stitches before previously wrapped stitch, w&t.

Next row (RS): Knit to end of row.

Repeat these last 2 rows 3 more times.

Next row (WS): Purl to end of row, working all wrapped stitches with the stitch they wrap.*

Next row (RS): Knit.

Next row (WS): Purl.

We are now switching to reverse stockinette stitch.

Next row (RS): P1, M1P, purl to end of row.

Next row (WS): Knit.

Repeat these last 2 rows 9 (9, 10, 11, 12, 13, 13, 13, 13) more times—118 (122, 124, 126, 128, 130, 132, 134, 134) stitches.

Break yarn.

Complete Right Side
The back and front stitches are now joined together and worked in one long row.

Joining Row (RS): Purl all back stitches, purl all front stitches (*using yarn from back stitches*)—236 (244, 248, 252, 256, 260, 264, 268, 268) stitches.

****Next row (WS):** Knit all stitches.

Work in pattern established for 12 (12, 12, 12, 14, 16, 18, 22, 24) more rows.

Double-Stitch Row (RS): Purl all stitches, wrapping yarn around right needle twice before pulling needle through stitch.

Drop-Stitch Row (WS): Knit all stitches, dropping extra yarn loop from needle as you knit.

Next row (RS): Purl.

Next row (WS): Knit.

Repeat these 4 rows once.**

Now work the back and front sections separately.

Right Back Side
We are now switching to stockinette stitch.

Dividing Row (RS): K88 (92, 94, 95, 96, 98, 102, 104, 106) stitches with second (shorter) circular needle; remaining stitches will be held on first (longer) needle until later.

Armhole Dec Row (WS): P2, ssp, purl to end of row.

Armhole Dec Row (RS): Knit to last 4 stitches, ssk, k2.

Repeat these 2 rows 0 (1, 2, 2, 2, 3, 3, 4, 4) more time(s)—86 (88, 88, 89, 90, 90, 94, 94, 96) stitches.

Next row (WS): Purl all stitches.

Work right-side armhole dec row.

Work these 2 rows 0 (2, 2, 3, 3, 3, 5, 5, 7) more times—85 (85, 85, 85, 86, 86, 88, 88, 88) stitches.

Work 1 (1, 3, 5, 7, 7, 7, 7, 7) row(s) even in stockinette stitch, ending with a wrong-side row.

Work short rows as for Right Back from * to *.

Break yarn, setting stitches aside using shorter circular needle as holder.

Right Front Side

With the right side facing, slip first 60 (60, 60, 62, 64, 64, 60, 60, 56) stitches onto holder for sleeve cap, rejoin yarn and knit remaining 88 (92, 94, 95, 96, 98, 102, 104, 106) stitches.

Armhole Dec Row (WS): Purl to last 4 stitches, p2tog, p2.

Armhole Dec Row (RS): K2, k2tog, knit to end of row.

Repeat these 2 rows 0 (1, 2, 2, 2, 3, 3, 4, 4) more time(s)—86 (88, 88, 89, 90, 90, 94, 94, 96) stitches.

Next row (WS): Purl all stitches.

Work right-side armhole dec row.

Work these 2 rows 0 (2, 2, 3, 3, 3, 5, 5, 7) more times—85 (85, 85, 85, 86, 86, 88, 88, 88) stitches.

Work 1 (1, 3, 5, 7, 7, 7, 7, 7) row(s) even in stockinette stitch, ending with a wrong-side row.

Work short rows as for Right Front from * to *.

Joining Row: Fold front and back of sweater together with the wrong sides touching each other and the right side facing you. Using three-needle bind-off, bind off all 85 (85, 85, 85, 86, 86, 88, 88, 88) stitches.

Note: The bind-off is made on the right side of the work so it will be visible on the right side.

LEFT SIDE

Left Back

With wrong side of Right Back cast-on facing you and starting at the hem, using shorter circular needle, pick up and knit 114 (118, 120, 122, 124, 126, 128, 130, 130) stitches.

***Next row (RS):** Knit.

Short Row 1 (WS): P74, w&t.

Next row (RS): Knit to end of row.

Short Row 2 (WS): Purl to 14 stitches before previously wrapped stitch, w&t.

Next row (RS): Knit to end of row.

Repeat these last 2 rows 3 more times.

Next row (WS): Purl to end of row, working all wrapped stitches with the stitch they wrap.*

Next row (RS): Knit.

Next row (WS): Purl.

We are now switching to reverse stockinette stitch.

Next row (RS): Purl.

Next row (WS): Knit.

Work 14 (14, 16, 18, 20, 22, 22, 22, 22) more rows in pattern established (reverse stockinette stitch).

Neck Inc Row (RS): P1, M1P, purl to end of row.

Neck Inc Row (WS): Knit to last 2 stitches, M1, k1.

Repeat these 2 rows once more—118 (122, 124, 126, 128, 130, 132, 134, 134) stitches.

Set stitches aside and break yarn.

Left Front

The top of the front will be open, so start picking up stitches partway down the right front cast-on, and cast on extra stitches to match the right front on the next wrong-side row.

Using longer circular needle, with wrong side of Right Front cast-on facing you and starting 14 (14, 16, 16, 16, 18, 18, 20, 20) stitches down at the neck, pick up and knit 94 (98, 97, 98, 99, 98, 100, 100, 100) stitches.

Note: As for the back seam, stitches are picked up deliberately on the right side of the work to create an exposed seam.

Next row (RS): Knit.

Next row (WS): Using knitted cast-on, cast on 14 (14, 16, 16, 16, 18, 18, 20, 20) stitches, purl to end of row—108 (112, 113, 114, 115, 116, 118, 120, 120) stitches.

*Short Row 1 (RS):** K74, w&t.

Next row (WS): Purl to end of row.

Short Row 2 (RS): Knit to 14 stitches before previously wrapped stitch, w&t.

Next row (WS): Purl to end of row.

Repeat these last 2 rows 3 more times.

Next row (RS): Knit to end of row, working all wrapped stitches with the stitch they wrap.

Next row (WS): Purl.*

We are now switching to reverse stockinette stitch.

Next row (RS): Purl to last stitch, M1P, p1.

Next row (WS): Knit.

Repeat these last 2 rows 9 (9, 10, 11, 12, 13, 13, 13, 13) more times—118 (122, 124, 126, 128, 130, 132, 134, 134) stitches. Do not break yarn.

Complete Left Side

Joining Row (RS): Purl all front stitches, purl all back stitches (*using yarn from front stitches*)—236 (244, 248, 252, 256, 260, 264, 268, 268) stitches.

From here, work as for Complete Right Side from ** to **.

Left Front Side
We are now switching to stockinette stitch.

Dividing Row (RS): K88 (92, 94, 95, 96, 98, 102, 104, 106) stitches with second (shorter) circular needle, remaining stitches will be held on first (longer) needle until later.

Armhole Dec Row (WS): P2, ssp, purl to end of row.

Armhole Dec Row (RS): Knit to last 4 stitches, ssk, k2.

Repeat these last 2 rows 0 (1, 2, 2, 2, 3, 3, 4, 4) more time(s)—86 (88, 88, 89, 90, 90, 94, 94, 96) stitches.

Next row (WS): Purl all stitches.

Work right-side armhole dec row.

Work these last 2 rows 0 (2, 2, 3, 3, 3, 5, 5, 7) more times—85 (85, 85, 85, 86, 86, 88, 88, 88) stitches.

Work 1 (1, 3, 5, 7, 7, 7, 7, 7) row(s) even in stockinette stitch, ending with a wrong-side row.

Work short rows as for Left Front from * to *.

Break yarn and set stitches aside, using circular needle as holder.

Left Back Side
With the right side of work facing, slip first 60 (60, 60, 62, 64, 64, 60, 60, 56) stitches onto holder for sleeve cap, rejoin yarn, and knit remaining 88 (92, 94, 95, 96, 98, 102, 104, 106) stitches.

Armhole Dec Row (WS): Purl to last 4 stitches, p2tog, p2.

Armhole Dec Row (RS): K2, k2tog, knit to end of row.

Repeat these last 2 rows 0 (1, 2, 2, 2, 3, 3, 4, 4) more time(s)—86 (88, 88, 89, 90, 90, 94, 94, 96) stitches.

Next row (WS): Purl all stitches.

Work right-side armhole dec row.

Work these last 2 rows 0 (2, 2, 3, 3, 3, 5, 5, 7) more times—85 (85, 85, 85, 86, 86, 88, 88, 88) stitches.

Work 1 (1, 3, 5, 7, 7, 7, 7, 7) row(s) even in stockinette stitch, ending with a wrong-side row.

Work short rows as for Left Back from * to *.

Joining Row: Fold front and back of sweater together with the wrong sides touching each other and the right side facing you. Using three-needle bind-off, bind off all 85 (85, 85, 85, 86, 86, 88, 88, 88) stitches.

SLEEVES
Short Row Cap
With the right side of work facing and starting at center of underarm using longer circular needle for Magic Loop (or double-pointed needles), pick up and knit 5 (9, 12, 14, 16, 17, 20, 21, 24) stitches to edge of held stitches, knit all 60 (60, 60, 62, 64, 64, 60, 60, 56) held stitches, pick up and knit remaining 5 (9, 12, 14, 16, 17, 20, 21, 24) stitches to center of underarm, place marker for start of round—70 (78, 84, 90, 96, 98, 100, 102, 104) stitches.

Short Row Setup (RS): K47 (51, 55, 58, 62, 63, 64, 65, 66) stitches, w&t.

Short Row Setup (WS): P24 (24, 26, 26, 28, 28, 28, 28, 28) stitches, w&t.

Short Row: Work to previously wrapped stitch, work wrap with stitch it wraps, w&t.

Work this last row 39 (41, 45, 47, 51, 53, 55, 57, 59) more times.

Knit to end of round, picking up final wraps and working them with the stitch they wrap.

Arm
Knit 10 (8, 6, 6, 6, 6, 6, 6, 6) rounds.

Sleeve Dec Rnd: K2tog, work to last 2 stitches, ssk—68 (76, 82, 88, 94, 96, 98, 100, 102) stitches; 2 stitches decreased.

Repeat these 11 (9, 7, 7, 7, 7, 7, 7, 7) rounds 6 (8, 11, 12, 12, 13, 13, 13, 13) more times—56 (60, 60, 64, 70, 70, 72, 74, 76) stitches.

Work even in stockinette stitch until sleeve measures 11½ (11½, 12, 12, 12½, 12½, 13, 13, 13½)" (29 [29, 30.5, 30.5, 32, 32, 33, 33, 34.5]cm) from end of short-row cap or desired length. Bind off all stitches.

Repeat for second sleeve.

FINISHING

Weave in all loose ends. Block garment to dimensions given on schematic.

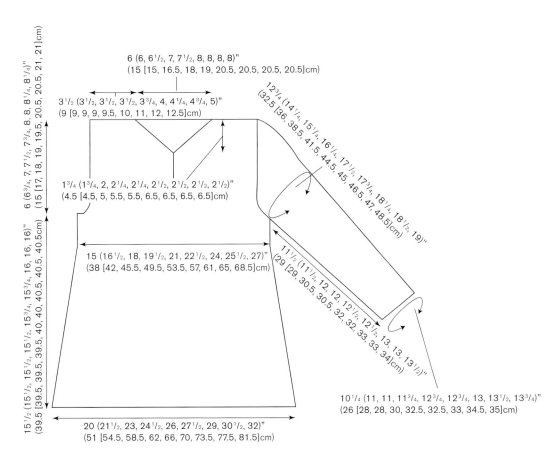

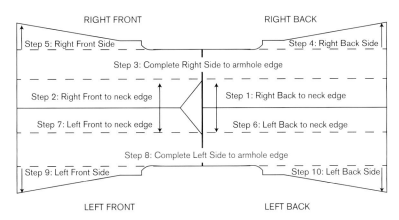

salto

SET-IN SLEEVE CARDIGAN

The delicate pattern in this cardigan is subtle but elegant, and the increases and decreases mimic cables but create a much more flexible fabric than a true cable. This cardigan is knit flat in one piece from the bottom up, and short rows are used at the top of the shoulders to create the shoulder slope. When the body is finished, set-in sleeves are worked from the top down using short rows to shape the sleeve cap.

Skill Level Intermediate

Sizes and Finished Measurements

To Fit Bust Circumference (up to)	31" (79cm)	34" (86cm)	37" (94cm)	40½" (103cm)	43½" (110.5cm)	45½" (115.5cm)	49" (124.5cm)	52" (132cm)	55½" (141cm)
Bust Size	32" (81cm)	35" (89cm)	38" (96.5cm)	41½" (105.5cm)	44½" (113cm)	46½" (118cm)	50" (127cm)	53" (134.5cm)	56½" (143.5cm)
Length	22¾" (58cm)	23¼" (59cm)	23¾" (60.5cm)	24" (61cm)	24¼" (61.5cm)	25¼" (64cm)	25½" (65cm)	25¾" (65.5cm)	26¼" (67cm)

Size 35" (89cm) modeled with 1½" (3.8cm) of positive ease

Materials

YARN

5 (5, 6, 6, 6, 7, 7, 8, 8) skeins Hedgehog Fibres Blue Faced DK, 100% Blue Faced Leicester wool, 3.53 oz (100g), 246 yd (225m), in Wish **3** light

NEEDLES & NOTIONS

1 US size 6 (4mm) circular needle, 40" (101.5cm) long, for body (or longer for larger sizes)
Set of US size 6 (4mm) double-pointed needles for sleeves
Adjust needle size as necessary to achieve gauge.
Stitch markers

(continues)

NEEDLES & NOTIONS (continued)

Stitch holders or waste yarn

5 lockable stitch markers

5 buttons, 1" (2.5cm) diameter

Tapestry needle

Gauge

20 stitches and 27 rows = 4" (10cm) in stockinette stitch, blocked

22 stitches and 27 rows = 4" (10cm) in lace pattern, blocked

Short Row Method Used

Wrap and Turn (page 10)

Techniques

For other techniques used in the pattern, please refer to General Techniques (page 155).

LACE PATTERN

(multiple of 18 [20] stitches for Small [Large] chart)

LACE CHART

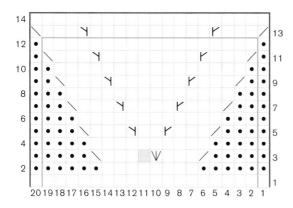

Row 1 (RS): K18 (20).

Row 2 (WS): K5 (6), p8, k5 (6).

Row 3 (RS): P4 (5), k2tog, k3, M2, k3, ssk, p4 (5).

Row 4 (WS): K4 (5), p10, k4 (5).

Row 5 (RS): P3 (4), k2tog, k3, M1R, k2, M1L, k3, ssk, p3 (4).

Row 6 (WS): K3 (4), p12, k3 (4).

Row 7 (RS): P2 (3), k2tog, k3, M1R, k4, M1L, k3, ssk, p2 (3).

Row 8 (WS): K2 (3), p14, k2 (3).

Row 9 (RS): P1 (2), k2tog, k3, M1R, k6, M1L, k3, ssk, p1 (2).

Row 10 (WS): K1 (2), p16, k1 (2).

Row 11 (RS): P0 (1), k2tog, k3, M1R, k8, M1L, k3, ssk, p0 (1).

Row 12 (WS): K0 (1), p18, k0 (1).

SIZE LARGE ONLY:

Row 13 (RS): K2tog, k3, M1R, k10, M1L, k3, ssk.

Row 14 (WS): P20.

Repeat rows 1–12 (14) for lace pattern.

I-CORD BUTTONHOLE

Work to buttonhole position in I-cord bind-off, slip 3 I-cord stitches from left to right needle, slip next 2 stitches from left to right needle, pass second stitch over first, *slip next stitch from left to right needle, pass second stitch over first again, repeat from * once. Slip stitch back from right to left needle.

*Slip 3 I-cord stitches from right to left needle, k3; repeat from * twice.

Resume I-cord bind-off until next buttonhole position.

BODY

Using longer circular needle, cast on 174 (190, 206, 222, 238, 250, 266, 282, 298) stitches.

Ribbing Row 1 (RS): K1, *k1, p1; repeat from * to last stitch, k1.

Ribbing Row 2 (WS): P1, *k1, p1; repeat from * to last stitch, p1.

Work these 2 rows until ribbing measures 1½" (3.8cm), ending with a wrong-side row.

Setup Row (RS): K1, work Small (Small, Small, Small, Large, Large, Large, Large, Large) lace pattern twice, place dart marker, k7 (11, 15, 19, 19, 22, 26, 30, 34), place marker for side seam, k7 (11, 15, 19, 19, 22, 26, 30, 34), place dart marker, work Small (Small, Small, Small, Large, Large, Large, Large, Large) lace pattern 4 times, place dart marker, k7 (11, 15, 19, 19, 22, 26, 30, 34), place marker for side seam, k7 (11, 15, 19, 19, 22, 26, 30, 34), place dart marker, work Small (Small, Small, Small, Large, Large, Large, Large, Large) lace pattern twice, k1.

Work next wrong-side row in pattern established, working stitches outside lace pattern in stockinette stitch.

Waist Dec Row (RS): *Work in pattern to dart marker, slip marker, k2tog, work in pattern to 2 stitches before next dart marker, ssk, slip marker; repeat from * once, work in pattern to end of row—4 stitches decreased.

Work waist dec row every 6 rows 4 more times—154 (170, 186, 202, 218, 230, 246, 262, 278) stitches.

Work 11 rows even in pattern.

Bust Inc Row (RS): Work in pattern to dart marker, slip marker, M1L, work in pattern to next dart marker, M1R, slip marker; repeat from * once, work in pattern to end of row—4 stitches increased.

Work bust inc row every 8 rows 4 more times—174 (190, 206, 222, 238, 250, 266, 282, 298) stitches.

Remove all dart markers.

Work even in pattern until body measures 14½ (14½, 14½, 14½, 14½, 15, 15, 15, 15)" (37 [37, 37, 37, 37, 38, 38, 38, 38]cm) from cast-on edge, ending with a wrong-side row.

Dividing Row (RS): *Work in pattern to 2 (3, 4, 5, 6, 6, 8, 10, 12) stitches before side seam, bind off 4 (6, 8, 10, 12, 12, 16, 20, 24) stitches, removing side seam marker; repeat from * once more, work in pattern to end of row.

Slip 42 (45, 48, 51, 54, 57, 59, 61, 63) stitches from each end onto the working needle; remaining 82 (88, 94, 100, 106, 112, 116, 120, 124) stitches for the back are placed on stitch holder or waste yarn to be worked later.

FRONT
Both sides of the front will be worked at the same time with 2 separate balls of yarn. Instructions for each side are divided by a semicolon.

Neck shaping happens at the same time as armhole shaping, starting on the first right-side row. Read through complete instructions and work both at the same time.

Join new yarn to right front stitches; yarn is still attached to left front stitches.

Armhole Shaping
Note: Armhole shaping is worked at same time as neck shaping.

Armhole Dec Row (WS): P1, ssp, work in pattern to end of right front; work left front to last 3 stitches, p2tog, p1—1 stitch decreased each side.

Armhole Dec Row (RS): K1, k2tog, work in pattern to end of left front; work right front to last 3 stitches, ssk, k1—1 stitch decreased each side.

Repeat these 2 rows 0 (0, 0, 1, 1, 1, 1, 2, 2) more time(s).

Next row (WS): Work all stitches even in pattern.

Work right-side armhole dec row.

Repeat these last 2 rows 1 (4, 6, 6, 6, 6, 7, 6, 7) more time(s).

Neck Shaping
Note: Neck shaping is worked at same time as armhole shaping.

Neck Dec Row (RS): Work in pattern to last 21 (21, 21, 21, 23, 23, 23, 23, 23) stitches, k2tog, place marker, work in pattern to end of left front; work 19 (19, 19, 19, 21, 21, 21, 21, 21) stitches in pattern, place marker, ssk, work in pattern to end of right front.

Note: Only one lace pattern repeat remains on each front.

Work neck dec row every right-side row 12 (11, 9, 8, 11, 10, 10, 9, 8) more times and then every other right-side row 5 (6, 8, 9, 8, 9, 9, 10, 11) times—20 (20, 21, 22, 23, 26, 27, 28, 29) stitches each side.

Work even in pattern until work measures 6¾ (7¼, 7¾, 8, 8¼, 8½, 8¾, 9, 9¼)" (17 [18.5, 19.5, 20.5, 21, 21.5, 22, 23, 23.5]cm) from dividing row, ending with a wrong-side row.

Shoulder Shaping

Short Row 1 (RS): Knit left side; knit to last 4 stitches, w&t.

Short Row 2 (WS): Purl right side; purl to last 4 stitches, w&t.

Short Row 3 (RS): Knit left side; knit to 4 stitches before previously wrapped stitch, w&t.

Short Row 4 (WS): Purl right side; purl to 4 stitches before previously wrapped stitch, w&t.

Work short rows 3 and 4 as above 2 (2, 2, 2, 2, 3, 3, 3, 4) more times.

Next row (RS): Work left side; k2tog, work to end of right side, picking up all wraps and working them with the stitch they wrap.

Next row (WS): Work right side; p2tog, work to end of left side, picking up all wraps and working them with the stitch they wrap—19 (19, 20, 21, 22, 25, 26, 27, 28) stitches each side.

Hold stitches on stitch holders or waste yarn to be worked later.

BACK

Join yarn to back stitches, starting with a wrong-side row.

Armhole Dec Row (WS): P1, ssp, work in pattern to last 3 stitches, p2tog, p1.

Armhole Dec Row (RS): K1, k2tog, work in pattern to last 3 stitches, ssk, k1.

Repeat these 2 rows 0 (0, 0, 1, 1, 1, 1, 2, 2) more times.

Next row (WS): Work all stitches even in pattern.

Work right-side armhole dec row.

Repeat these last 2 rows 1 (4, 6, 6, 6, 6, 7, 6, 7) more time(s)—74 (74, 76, 78, 84, 90, 92, 94, 96) stitches.

Note: For some sizes, the last few armhole decreases will disrupt the edge of the chart; ensure you have the correct stitch count.

Work even in pattern until work measures 6¾ (7¼, 7¾, 8, 8¼, 8½, 8¾, 9, 9¼)" (17 [18.5, 19.5, 20.5, 21, 21.5, 22, 23, 23.5]cm), ending with a wrong-side row.

Shoulder Shaping

Short Row 1 (RS): Knit to last 4 stitches, w&t.

Short Row 2 (WS): Purl to last 4 stitches, w&t.

Short Row 3 (RS): Knit to 4 stitches before previously wrapped stitch, w&t.

Short Row 4 (WS): Purl to 4 stitches before previously wrapped stitch, w&t.

Work short rows 3 and 4 as above 0 (0, 0, 0, 0, 1, 1, 1, 2) more time(s).

Place removable marker at each side of center 28 (28, 28, 28, 32, 32, 32, 32, 32) stitches.

Neck Bind-Off Row (RS): Knit to 4 stitches before removable marker, ssk, k2, remove marker, with second ball of yarn, bind off 28 (28, 28, 28, 32, 32, 32, 32) stitches, remove marker, k2, k2tog, knit to 4 stitches before previously wrapped stitch, w&t.

Each side of the back is now worked separately with different balls of yarn. Each side is shown divided with a semicolon.

Neck Dec Row (WS): Purl to 4 stitches before neck, p2tog, p2; p2, ssp, purl to 4 stitches before previously wrapped stitch, w&t.

Neck Dec Row (RS): Knit to 4 stitches before neck, ssk, k2; k2, k2tog, knit to 4 stitches before previously wrapped stitch, w&t.

Work 1 more wrong-side neck dec row—19 (19, 20, 21, 22, 25, 26, 27, 28) stitches.

Work to end of right-side row, picking up all wraps and working them with the stitch they wrap.

Work 1 more wrong-side row, picking up all wraps and working them with the stitch they wrap.

Turn garment inside out so the right sides of front and back are facing each other. Using three-needle bind-off, join the 19 (19, 20, 21, 22, 25, 26, 27, 28) stitches from front and back of the right and left shoulders together.

SLEEVES

Sleeves are worked in the round with long circular needle using the Magic Loop; alternatively you may use double-pointed needles.

Sleeve Cap

With longer circular needle and right side facing, start at center of underarm cast-on stitches and pick up and knit 28 (30, 31, 32, 33, 36, 38, 41, 43) stitches to top of shoulder, pick up and knit 28 (30, 31, 32, 33, 36, 38, 41, 43) stitches from top of shoulder to center of underarm cast-on stitches, place marker for start of round—56 (60, 62, 64, 66, 72, 76, 82, 86) stitches.

Short Row 1 (RS): K19 (21, 22, 23, 24, 27, 29, 32, 34) stitches, work Small lace pattern, k0 (0, 0, 0, 0, 1, 1, 1, 1), w&t.

Short Row 2 (WS): P0 (0, 0, 0, 0, 1, 1, 1, 1), work Small lace pattern, p0 (0, 0, 0, 0, 1, 1, 1, 1), w&t.

Short Row 3 (RS): Work in pattern to previously wrapped stitch, knit stitch (*do not lift wrap*), w&t.

Short Row 4 (WS): Work in pattern to previously wrapped stitch, purl stitch (*do not lift wrap*), w&t.

Work short rows 3 and 4 as above 15 (16, 17, 18, 20, 21, 22, 23, 23) more times.

Next Row (RS): Knit to end of round.

Note: It is not necessary to pick up wraps as you pass them; they create a "seam line" at the edge of the sleeve cap.

Arm

Work in pattern for 14 (11, 11, 10, 10, 8, 7, 6, 5) rounds.

Sleeve Dec Rnd: K2tog, work to last 2 stitches, ssk—2 stitches decreased.

Work sleeve dec rnd every 15 (12, 12, 11, 11, 9, 8, 7, 6) rounds 6 (8, 8, 9, 9, 12, 13, 15, 17) more times—42 (42, 44, 44, 46, 46, 48, 50, 50) stitches.

Work even in pattern until sleeve measures 16½ (17, 17, 17, 17½, 17½, 17½, 18, 18)" (42 [43, 43, 43, 44.5, 44.5, 44.5, 45.5, 45.5]cm) from underarm.

Ribbing Rnd: *K1, p1; repeat from * to end of round.

Work ribbing rnd until cuff measures 1½" (3.8cm).

Bind off all stitches loosely in pattern.

Repeat for other sleeve.

FINISHING

I-Cord Edging

With right side facing and using circular needle, start at the bottom right front and pick up and knit 3 stitches for every 4 rows, or 1 stitch for every bound-off stitch, until all stitches to bottom of left front have been picked up. Break yarn.

Using lockable stitch markers, evenly space and mark location of 5 buttons along right front, starting 3 stitches from bottom and ending where neckline begins to slope.

Slip stitches to right end of the needle, rejoin yarn and work I-cord bind-off, making I-cord buttonhole at every stitch marker location.

Weave in all loose ends. Block garment to dimensions given on schematic.

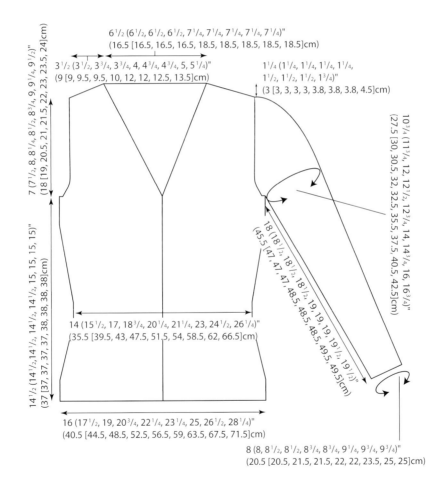

6¹/₂ (6¹/₂, 6¹/₂, 6¹/₂, 7¹/₄, 7¹/₄, 7¹/₄, 7¹/₄, 7¹/₄)"
(16.5 [16.5, 16.5, 16.5, 18.5, 18.5, 18.5, 18.5, 18.5]cm)

3¹/₂ (3¹/₂, 3³/₄, 3³/₄, 4, 4³/₄, 4³/₄, 5, 5¹/₄)"
(9 [9, 9.5, 9.5, 10, 12, 12, 12.5, 13.5]cm)

1¹/₄ (1¹/₄, 1¹/₄, 1¹/₄, 1¹/₄, 1¹/₂, 1¹/₂, 1¹/₂, 1³/₄)"
(3 [3, 3, 3, 3, 3.8, 3.8, 3.8, 4.5]cm)

7 (7¹/₂, 8, 8¹/₄, 8¹/₂, 8³/₄, 9, 9¹/₄, 9¹/₂)"
(18 [19, 20.5, 21, 21.5, 22, 23, 23.5, 24]cm)

10³/₄ (11³/₄, 12, 12¹/₂, 12³/₄, 14, 14³/₄, 16, 16³/₄)"
(27.5 [30, 30.5, 32, 32.5, 35.5, 37.5, 40.5, 42.5]cm)

14¹/₂ (14¹/₂, 14¹/₂, 14¹/₂, 15, 15, 15, 15)"
(37 [37, 37, 37, 38, 38, 38, 38]cm)

14 (15¹/₂, 17, 18³/₄, 20¹/₄, 21¹/₄, 23, 24¹/₂, 26¹/₄)"
(35.5 [39.5, 43, 47.5, 51.5, 54, 58.5, 62, 66.5]cm)

18 (18¹/₂, 18¹/₂, 18¹/₂, 19, 19, 19, 19¹/₂, 19¹/₂)"
(45.5 [47, 47, 47, 48.5, 48.5, 48.5, 49.5, 49.5]cm)

16 (17¹/₂, 19, 20³/₄, 22¹/₄, 23¹/₄, 25, 26¹/₂, 28¹/₄)"
(40.5 [44.5, 48.5, 52.5, 56.5, 59, 63.5, 67.5, 71.5]cm)

8 (8, 8¹/₂, 8¹/₂, 8³/₄, 8³/₄, 9¹/₄, 9³/₄, 9³/₄)"
(20.5 [20.5, 21.5, 21.5, 22, 22, 23.5, 25, 25]cm)

estrella

CARDIGAN WITH BUST SHAPING

Wide reversible cables dominate this cardigan, creating an elegant, dramatic statement. The cardigan is knit in one piece from the bottom up, with set-in sleeves worked from the top down. Short row bust shaping, with suggestions for different cup sizes, is included, creating a dressed-up, figure-flattering silhouette.

Skill Level Intermediate

Sizes and Finished Measurements

To Fit Bust Circumference (up to)	31½" (80cm)	34½" (87.5cm)	37½" (95.5cm)	40½" (103cm)	43½" (110.5cm)	46½" (118cm)	49½" (125.5cm)	52½" (133.5cm)	55½" (141cm)
Bust Size	32" (81cm)	35" (89cm)	38" (96.5cm)	41" (104cm)	44" (112cm)	47" (119.5cm)	50" (127cm)	53" (134.5cm)	56" (142cm)
Length	22¾" (58cm)	23¼" (59cm)	23¾" (60cm)	24¼" (61.5cm)	24¾" (63cm)	25" (63.5cm)	26" (66cm)	26¼" (67cm)	26½" (67.5cm)

Length does not include collar.
Size 35" (89cm) modeled with ½" (13mm) of positive ease and small bust darts

Materials

YARN

10 (10, 11, 12, 13, 14, 15, 16, 17) skeins O-Wool Classic Worsted, 100% organic merino, 3.53 oz (100g), 99 yd (90m), in Ash (9103) (**4**) medium
Note: Yarn used assumes smallest bust shaping; add extra yarn for larger bust sizes.

NEEDLES & NOTIONS

2 US size 8 (5mm) circular needles, 40" (101.5cm) long, for body (or longer for larger sizes)
Set of US size 8 (5mm) double-pointed needles for sleeves
Adjust needle size as necessary to achieve gauge.
Cable needle
Stitch markers

(continues)

NEEDLES & NOTIONS (continued)

Stitch holders or waste yarn

Safety pins for Japanese short rows

6 hook-and-eye closures

Tapestry needle

Gauge

16 stitches and 22 rows = 4" (10cm) in stockinette stitch, blocked

Braided cable measures 2" (5cm) across

Short Row Method Used

Japanese (page 14)

Techniques

For other techniques used in the pattern, please refer to General Techniques (page 155).

CABLES

6/6 LC: Slip the first 6 stitches onto the cable needle and hold at the front of the work, work the next 6 stitches in pattern, work the 6 held stitches in pattern.

6/6 RC: Slip the first 6 stitches onto the cable needle and hold at the back of the work, work the next 6 stitches in pattern, work the 6 held stitches in pattern.

BRAIDED CABLE (WORKED OVER 18 STITCHES)

This cable is reversible so it is worked in ribbing, which allows the cable to show on the back as well as the front. You will work stitches as knit or purl, depending on how they present; every time the cables cross, the knits and purls change position.

Setup Row (RS): *P2, k2; repeat from * 3 more times, p2.

Setup Row (WS): * K2, p2; repeat from * 3 more times, k2.

Row 1 (RS): 6/6 LC, work 6 stitches in pattern as presented.

Rows 2–8: Work all stitches in pattern as presented.

Row 9 (RS): Work 6 stitches in pattern as presented, 6/6 RC.

Rows 10–16: Work all stitches in pattern presented.

Repeat rows 1–16 for braided cable pattern.

Pattern Notes

- When choosing the bust size, refer to the techniques section on horizontal bust darts (Shaping Bust Darts, page 93).
- The first stitch of every row should be slipped for a smooth edge. On the right side, slip the first stitch knitwise with the yarn in the back; on the wrong side, slip the first stitch purlwise with the yarn in the front.

BODY

Using circular needle, cast on 152 (164, 176, 188, 200, 212, 224, 236, 248) stitches.

Slip the first stitch of every row as described above in Pattern Notes.

Ribbing Row (RS): K1, *p2, k2; repeat from * to last 3 stitches, p2, k1.

Ribbing Row (WS): P1, *k2, p2; repeat from * to last 3 stitches, k2, p1.

Work these 2 rows until ribbing measures 2" (5cm), ending with a wrong-side row.

Setup Row (RS): K1, Work braided cable, place marker, k2tog, k7 (7, 10, 12, 13, 15, 16, 18, 19), place dart marker, k16 (19, 19, 20, 22, 23, 25, 26, 28), place marker for side seam, k21 (23, 25, 27, 29, 31, 33, 35, 37), place dart marker, k22 (24, 26, 28, 30, 32, 34, 36, 38), place dart marker, k21 (23, 25, 27, 29, 31, 33, 35, 37), place marker for side seam, k16 (19, 19, 20, 22, 23, 25, 26, 28) place dart marker, k7 (7, 10, 12, 13, 15, 16, 18, 19), k2tog, work braided cable, k1—150 (162, 174, 186, 198, 210, 222, 234, 246) stitches.

Next row (WS): P1, work braided cable, purl to braided cable, work braided cable to last stitch, p1.

Work 2 rows even in pattern.

Waist Dec Row (RS): *Work in pattern to dart marker, slip marker, k2tog, work in pattern to 2 stitches before next dart marker, ssk, slip marker; repeat from * once, work in pattern to end of row—4 stitches decreased.

Work waist dec row every 4 rows 3 more times—134 (146, 158, 170, 182, 194, 206, 218, 230) stitches.

Work 9 rows even in pattern.

Bust Inc Row (RS): *Work in pattern to dart marker, slip marker, M1L, work in pattern to next dart marker, M1R, slip marker; repeat from * once, work in pattern to end of row—4 stitches increased.

Work bust inc row every 10 rows 3 more times—150 (162, 174, 186, 198, 210, 222, 234, 246) stitches.

Remove all dart markers.

Work even until work measures 12½ (12½, 12½, 12½, 12¾, 12¾, 13, 13, 13)" (32 [32, 32, 32, 32.5, 32.5, 33, 33, 33]cm) from cast-on edge, ending with a wrong-side row.

Short Row Bust Shaping

If the difference between your front and back length is less than 3" (7.5cm), omit bust shaping and move on to next section, All Sizes (page 142). Use bust shaping that corresponds to the difference between your front and back length; sizes S (M, L) are suitable for differences up to 4 (5, 6)" (10, 12.5, 15]cm).

You will work each bust dart separately. Make sure to keep track of the braided cable rows for each side as you work.

Small

RIGHT DART
Short Row 1 (RS): Work in pattern to 2 (4, 6, 4, 6, 2, 4, 6, 3) stitches before side seam, turn work.

Next row (WS): Slip stitch, place safety pin, work in pattern to end of row.

Short Row 2 (RS): Work in pattern to 2 (2, 2, 3, 3, 4, 4, 4, 5) stitches before gap, turn work.

Next row (WS): Slip stitch, place safety pin, work in pattern to end of row.

Work these last 2 rows 4 more times.

Work right-side row in pattern to end of row, working all yarn loops with corresponding stitches as you pass them.

LEFT DART
Short Row 1 (WS): Work in pattern to 2 (4, 6, 4, 6, 2, 4, 6, 3) stitches before side seam, turn work.

Next row (RS): Slip stitch, place safety pin, work in pattern to end of row.

Short Row 2 (WS): Work in pattern to 2 (2, 2, 3, 3, 4, 4, 4, 5) stitches before gap, turn work.

Next row (RS): Slip stitch, place safety pin, work in pattern to end of row.

Work these last 2 rows 4 more times.

Medium

RIGHT DART

Short Row 1 (RS): Work in pattern to 5 (7, 2, 4, 6, 8, 3, 5, 7) stitches before side seam, turn work.

Next row (WS): Slip stitch, place safety pin, work in pattern to end of row.

Short Row 2 (RS): Work in pattern to 1 (1, 2, 2, 2, 2, 3, 3, 3) stitch(es) before gap, turn work.

Next row (WS): Slip stitch, place safety pin, work in pattern to end of row.

Work these last 2 rows 6 more times.

Work right-side row in pattern to end of row, working all yarn loops with corresponding stitches as you pass them.

LEFT DART

Short Row 1 (WS): Work in pattern to 5 (7, 2, 4, 6, 8, 3, 5, 7) stitches before side seam, turn work.

Next row (RS): Slip stitch, place safety pin, work in pattern to end of row.

Short Row 2 (WS): Work in pattern to 1 (1, 2, 2, 2, 2, 3, 3, 3) stitch(es) before gap, turn work.

Next row (RS): Slip stitch, place safety pin, work in pattern to end of row.

Work these last 2 rows 6 more times.

Large

RIGHT DART

Short Row 1 (RS): Work in pattern to 2 (4, 6, 8, 10, 2, 4, 6, 8) stitches before side seam, turn work.

Next row (WS): Slip stitch, place safety pin, work in pattern to end of row.

Short Row 2 (RS): Work in pattern to 1 (1, 1, 1, 1, 2, 2, 2, 2) stitch(es) before gap, turn work.

Next row (WS): Slip stitch, place safety pin, work in pattern to end of row.

Work these last 2 rows 9 more times.

Work right-side row in pattern to end of row, working all yarn loops with corresponding stitches as you pass them.

LEFT DART

Short Row 1 (WS): Work in pattern to 2 (4, 6, 8, 10, 2, 4, 6, 8) stitches before side seam, turn work.

Next row (RS): Slip stitch, place safety pin, work in pattern to end of row.

Short Row 2 (WS): Work in pattern to 1 (1, 1, 1, 1, 2, 2, 2, 2) stitch(es) before gap, turn work.

Next row (RS): Slip stitch, place safety pin, work in pattern to end of row.

Work these last 2 rows 9 more times.

All Sizes

Note: On next wrong-side row, take care to work all yarn loops with corresponding stitches as you pass them.

Work even in pattern until body measures 14½ (14½, 14½, 14½, 14¾, 14¾, 15, 15, 15)" (37 [37, 37, 37, 37.5, 37.5, 38, 38, 38]cm) from cast-on edge, ending with a wrong-side row. Be sure to measure at back so short rows are not included in length.

Dividing Row (RS): *Work in pattern to 2 (4, 5, 6, 6, 7, 7, 8, 9) stitches before side seam, bind off 4 (8, 10, 12, 12, 14, 14, 16, 18) stitches, removing side seam marker; repeat from * once more, work in pattern to end of row.

Slip 41 (42, 44, 46, 49, 51, 54, 56, 58) stitches from each end onto the working needle; remaining 60 (62, 66, 70, 76, 80, 86, 90, 94) stitches for the back are placed on stitch holder or waste yarn to be worked later.

FRONT
Both sides of the front will be worked at the same time with 2 separate balls of yarn. Instructions for each side are divided by a semicolon.

Neck shaping happens at the same time as armhole shaping, starting on the first right-side row. Read through complete instructions and work both at the same time.

Join new yarn to right front stitches; yarn is still attached to left front stitches.

Armhole Shaping
Note: This is worked at same time as neck shaping.

Armhole Dec Row (WS): P1, ssp, work in pattern to end of right front; work left front to last 3 stitches, p2tog, p1—1 stitch decreased each side.

Armhole Dec Row (RS): K1, k2tog, work in pattern to end of left front; work right front to last 3 stitches, ssk, k1—1 stitch decreased each side.

Repeat these 2 rows 0 (0, 0, 0, 0, 0, 1, 1, 1) more time(s).

Next row (WS): Work all stitches even in pattern.

Work right-side armhole dec row.

Repeat these last 2 rows 1 (2, 3, 4, 5, 5, 5, 6, 7) more time(s).

Neck Shaping
Note: This is worked at same time as armhole shaping.

Neck Dec Row (RS): Work in pattern to 2 stitches before cable marker, k2tog, slip marker, work braided cable to end of left front; work braided cable, slip marker, ssk, work in pattern to end of right front.

Work neck dec row every 8 (8, 8, 8, 6, 6, 6, 6, 6) rows 4 (4, 5, 5, 6, 7, 7, 8) more times—32 (32, 32, 33, 34, 35, 36, 36, 37) stitches each side.

Work even in pattern until work measures 6¾ (7¼, 7¾, 8, 8¼, 8½, 8¾, 9, 9¼)" (17 [18.5, 19.5, 20.5, 21, 21.5, 22, 23, 23.5]cm) from dividing row, ending with a wrong-side row.

Shoulders
Short Row 1 (RS): Work left side; work to last 3 stitches of right side, turn.

Short Row 2 (WS): Slip stitch, place safety pin, work right side; work to last 3 stitches of left side, turn.

Short Row 3 (RS): Slip stitch, place safety pin, work left side; knit to 3 stitches before gap on right side, turn.

Short Row 4 (WS): Slip stitch, place safety pin, work right side; work to 3 stitches before gap on left side, turn.

Work short rows 3 and 4 as above 1 (1, 1, 2, 2, 2, 3, 3, 3) more times.

Work 2 more rows, working all yarn loops with corresponding stitches as you pass them.

Hold stitches to be worked later on stitch holder or waste yarn.

BACK
Join yarn to back stitches, starting with a wrong-side row.

Armhole Dec Row (WS): P1, ssp, purl to last 3 stitches, p2tog, p1.

Armhole Dec Row (RS): K1, k2tog, knit to last 3 stitches, ssk, k1.

Repeat these 2 rows 0 (0, 0, 0, 0, 0, 1, 1, 1) more time(s).

Next row (WS): Purl all stitches.

Work right-side armhole dec row.

Repeat these 2 rows 1 (2, 3, 4, 5, 5, 5, 6, 7) more time(s)—52 (52, 54, 56, 60, 64, 66, 68, 70) stitches.

Work even in pattern until work measures 6¾ (7¼, 7¾, 8, 8¼, 8½, 8¾, 9, 9¼)" (17 [18.5, 19.5, 20.5, 21, 21.5, 22, 23, 23.5]cm), ending with a wrong-side row.

Shoulders
Neck Bind-Off Row (RS): K13 (13, 13, 14, 15, 16, 17, 17, 18), ssk, k2, with second ball of yarn, bind off 18 (18, 20, 20, 22, 24, 24, 26, 26) stitches, k1, k2tog, knit to last 3 stitches, turn.

Note: Each side of the back is now worked separately with 2 balls of yarn. Instructions for each side are divided by a semicolon.

Neck Dec Row (WS): Slip stitch, place safety pin, purl to 3 stitches before neck, p2tog, p2; p2, ssp, purl to last 3 stitches, turn.

Neck Dec Row (RS): Slip stitch, place safety pin, knit to 3 stitches before neck, ssk, k2; k2, k2tog, knit to 3 stitches before gap, turn.

Neck Dec Row (WS): Slip stitch, place safety pin, purl to 3 stitches before neck, p2tog, p2; p2, ssp, purl to 3 stitches before gap, turn—13 (13, 13, 14, 15, 16, 17, 17, 18) stitches each side.

Short Row 1 (RS): Slip stitch, place safety pin, knit to 3 stitches before gap, turn.

Short Row 2 (WS): Slip stitch, place safety pin, purl to 3 stitches before gap, turn.

Work short rows 1 and 2 as above 0 (0, 0, 1, 1, 1, 2, 2, 2) more time(s).

Work to end of right-side row, picking up all yarn loops and working them with the corresponding stitch.

Work 1 more wrong-side row, working all yarn loops with corresponding stitches as you pass them.

Turn garment inside out so the right sides of front and back are touching each other. Using three-needle bind-off, join the 13 (13, 13, 14, 15, 16, 17, 17, 18) stitches from front and back of the right and left shoulders together—19 edge stitches remain at each front.

SLEEVES
Sleeves are worked in the round with long circular needle using the Magic Loop method. Alternatively, you may use double-pointed needles.

Sleeve Cap
With circular needle and right side facing, start at center of underarm cast-on stitches and pick up and knit 23 (24, 25, 26, 27, 29, 31, 33, 35) stitches to top of shoulder, pick up and knit 23 (24, 25, 26, 27, 29, 31, 33, 35) stitches from top of shoulder to center of underarm cast-on stitches, place marker for start of round—46 (48, 50, 52, 54, 58, 62, 66, 70) stitches.

Short Row 1 (RS): K29 (30, 31, 32, 33, 36, 38, 40, 43), turn work.

Short Row 2 (WS): Slip stitch, place safety pin, p11 (11, 11, 11, 11, 13, 13, 13, 15), turn work.

Short Row 3 (RS): Slip stitch, place safety pin, knit to gap, work yarn loop with next stitch, turn work.

Short Row 4 (WS): Slip stitch, place safety pin, purl to gap, work yarn loop with next stitch, turn work.

Work short rows 3 and 4 as above 12 (12, 14, 15, 16, 17, 18, 19, 19) more times.

Next Row (RS): Knit to end of round.

Arm
Work in stockinette stitch for 15 (13, 11, 10, 11, 9, 7, 7, 6) rounds.

Sleeve Dec Rnd: K2tog, work to last 2 stitches, ssk—2 stitches decreased.

Work sleeve dec rnd every 16 (14, 12, 11, 12, 10, 8, 8, 7) rounds 4 (5, 6, 7, 6, 8, 10, 10, 12) more times—36 (36, 36, 36, 40, 40, 40, 44, 44) stitches.

Work even in pattern until sleeve measures 16 (16½, 16½, 16½, 17, 17, 17, 17½, 17½)" (40.5 [42, 42, 42, 43, 43, 43, 44.5, 44.5]cm) from underarm.

Ribbing Rnd: *K2, p2; repeat from * to end of round.

Work ribbing rnd until cuff measures 2" (5cm).

Bind off all stitches loosely in pattern.

Repeat for other sleeve.

FINISHING

Neck Edging

Rejoin yarn to each side of neck edging. Continue to work in pattern until edges meet with a gentle stretch at the back of the neck.

With wrong side of work facing, join both sides using a three-needle bind-off.

Sew neck edging to the back of the neck.

Sew 6 hooks and eyes at each side, starting at the bottom of the cardigan and ending where the neck starts to slope.

Weave in all loose ends. Block garment to dimensions given on schematic.

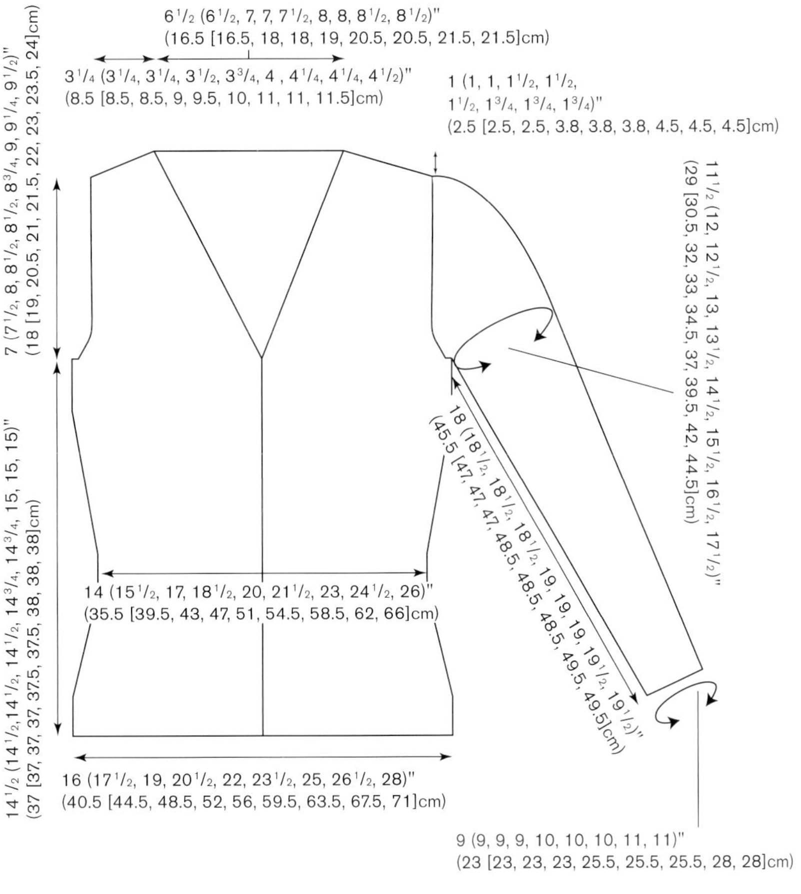
6 1/2 (6 1/2, 7, 7, 7 1/2, 8, 8, 8 1/2, 8 1/2)"
(16.5 [16.5, 18, 18, 19, 20.5, 20.5, 21.5, 21.5]cm)
3 1/4 (3 1/4, 3 1/4, 3 1/2, 3 3/4, 4 , 4 1/4, 4 1/4, 4 1/2)"
(8.5 [8.5, 8.5, 9, 9.5, 10, 11, 11, 11.5]cm)
1 (1, 1, 1 1/2, 1 1/2, 1 1/2, 1 3/4, 1 3/4, 1 3/4)"
(2.5 [2.5, 2.5, 3.8, 3.8, 3.8, 4.5, 4.5, 4.5]cm)
7 (7 1/2, 8, 8 1/2, 8 1/2, 8 3/4, 9, 9 1/4, 9 1/2)"
(18 [19, 20.5, 21, 21.5, 22, 23, 23.5, 24]cm)
11 1/2 (12, 12 1/2, 13, 13 1/2, 14 1/2, 15 1/2, 16 1/2, 17 1/2)"
(29 [30.5, 32, 33, 34.5, 37, 39.5, 42, 44.5]cm)
18 (18 1/2, 18 1/2, 18 1/2, 19, 19, 19, 19 1/2, 19 1/2)"
(45.5 [47, 47, 47, 48.5, 48.5, 48.5, 49.5, 49.5]cm)
14 (15 1/2, 17, 18 1/2, 20, 21 1/2, 23, 24 1/2, 26)"
(35.5 [39.5, 43, 47, 51, 54.5, 58.5, 62, 66]cm)
14 1/2 (14 1/2, 14 1/2, 14 1/2, 14 3/4, 14 3/4, 15, 15, 15)"
(37 [37, 37, 37.5, 37.5, 38, 38, 38, 38]cm)
16 (17 1/2, 19, 20 1/2, 22, 23 1/2, 25, 26 1/2, 28)"
(40.5 [44.5, 48.5, 52, 56, 59.5, 63.5, 67.5, 71]cm)
9 (9, 9, 9, 10, 10, 10, 11, 11)"
(23 [23, 23, 23, 25.5, 25.5, 25.5, 28, 28]cm)

Note: Bust darts and collar are not shown in schematic.

orosi

TOP-DOWN COWLED SWEATER

This cozy pullover will follow your curves for a very flattering fit, thanks to short rows added at the bust. Worked from the top down with raglan shoulder shaping, this sweater is a good opportunity to try out bust shaping. The short rows are located at each side of the central cable panel, so they are easily worked in stockinette stitch.

Skill Level Intermediate

Sizes and Finished Measurements

To Fit Bust Circumference (up to)	31¼" (79.5cm)	34" (86cm)	36¾" (93.5cm)	39½" (100cm)	42½" (108cm)	45¼" (115cm)	49" (124.5cm)	51¾" (131.5cm)	54¾" (139cm)
Bust Size	33" (84cm)	35¾" (91cm)	38½" (98cm)	41¼" (105cm)	44¼" (112.5cm)	47" (119.5cm)	50¾" (129cm)	53½" (136cm)	56½" (143.5cm)
Length	21½" (55cm)	22¼" (56.5cm)	22¾" (58cm)	23¼" (59cm)	24" (61cm)	24¼" (61.5cm)	25" (63.5cm)	25¼" (64cm)	25¼" (64cm)

Size 35¾" (91cm) modeled with 2½" (6.5cm) of positive ease and small bust darts

Materials

YARN

8 (9, 10, 10, 11, 11, 12, 13, 13) skeins Green Mountain Spinnery Mountain Mohair, 70% wool, 30% yearling mohair, 2 oz (57g), 140 yds (128m), in Alpenglo (7480) 〔4〕 medium

Note: Yarn used assumes smallest bust shaping; add extra yarn for larger bust sizes.

NEEDLES & NOTIONS

1 US size 8 (5mm) circular needle, 32" (81cm) long, for body (or longer for larger sizes)

1 US size 8 (5mm) circular needle, 16" (40.5cm) long, for cowl

1 set US size 8 (5mm) double-pointed needles

Adjust needle size as necessary to achieve gauge.

Stitch markers

Cable needle

(continues)

NEEDLES & NOTIONS (continued)

Waste yarn

Tapestry needle

Gauge

17 stitches and 25 rows = 4" (10cm) in stockinette stitch, blocked

Cable chart measures 7" (18cm) wide

Short Row Method Used

Wrap and Turn (page 10)

Techniques

For other techniques used in the pattern, please refer to General Techniques (page 155).

CABLES

2/1 LPC: Slip 2 stitches onto cable needle, hold to front of work, purl 1 stitch, knit 2 stitches from cable needle.

2/1 RPC: Slip 1 stitch onto cable needle, hold to back of work, knit 2 stitches, purl 1 stitch from cable needle.

3/2 LPC: Slip 3 stitches onto cable needle, hold to front of work, purl 2 stitches, knit 3 stitches from cable needle.

3/2 RPC: Slip 2 stitches onto cable needle, hold to back of work, knit 3 stitches, purl 2 stitches from cable needle.

3/3 LC Slip 3 stitches onto cable needle, hold to front of work, knit 3 stitches, knit 3 stitches from cable needle.

3/3 RC: Slip 3 stitches onto cable needle, hold to back of work, knit 3 stitches, knit 3 stitches from cable needle.

CABLE PATTERN (52 STITCHES)

Rnd 1: P5, k2, p5, k2, p2, k3, p4, k6, p4, k3, p2, k2, p5, k2, p5.

Rnd 2: P4, 2/1 RPC, p4, 2/1 RPC, p2, k3, p4, k6, p4, k3, p2, 2/1 LPC, p4, 2/1 LPC, p4.

Rnd 3: P4, k2, p5, k2, p3, k3, p4, k6, p4, k3, p3, k2, p5, k2, p4.

Rnd 4: P3, 2/1 RPC, p4, 2/1 RPC, p3, k3, p4, 3/3 LC, p4, k3, p3, 2/1 LPC, p4, 2/1 LPC, p3.

Rnd 5: P3, k2, p5, k2, p4, k3, p4, k6, p4, k3, p4, k2, p5, k2, p3.

CABLE CHART

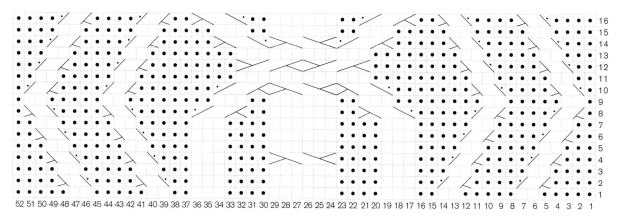

52 51 50 49 48 47 46 45 44 43 42 41 40 39 38 37 36 35 34 33 32 31 30 29 28 27 26 25 24 23 22 21 20 19 18 17 16 15 14 13 12 11 10 9 8 7 6 5 4 3 2 1

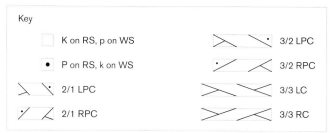

Key

	K on RS, p on WS
•	P on RS, k on WS
	2/1 LPC
	2/1 RPC
	3/2 LPC
	3/2 RPC
	3/3 LC
	3/3 RC

Rnd 6: P2, (2/1 RPC, p4) twice, k3, p4, k6, p4, k3, (p4, 2/1 LPC) twice, p2.

Rnd 7: P2, (k2, p5) twice, k3, p4, k6, p4, k3, (p5, k2) twice, p2.

Rnd 8: P1, 2/1 RPC, p4, 2/1 RPC, p5, 3/2 LPC, p2, k6, p2, 3/2 RPC, p5, 2/1 LPC, p4, 2/1 LPC, p1.

Rnd 9: P1, k2, p5, k2, p8, k3, p2, k6, p2, k3, p8, k2, p5, k2, p1.

Rnd 10: P1, 2/1 LPC, p4, 2/1 LPC, p7, 3/2 LPC, 3/3 LC, 3/2 RPC, p7, 2/1 RPC, p4, 2/1 RPC, p1.

Rnd 11: P2, k2, p5, k2, p9, k12, p9, k2, p5, k2, p2.

Rnd 12: P2, 2/1 LPC, p4, 2/1 LPC, p8, (3/3 RC) twice, p8, 2/1 RPC, p4, 2/1 RPC, p2.

Rnd 13: P3, k2, p5, k2, p8, k12, p8, k2, p5, k2, p3.

Rnd 14: P3, 2/1 LPC, p4, 2/1 LPC, p5, 3/2 RPC, 3/3 LC, 3/2 LPC, p5, 2/1 RPC, p4, 2/1 RPC, p3.

Rnd 15: P4, (k2, p5) twice, k3, p2, k6, p2, k3, (p5, k2) twice, p4.

Rnd 16: (P4, 2/1 LPC) twice, p2, 3/2 RPC, p2, k6, p2, 3/2 LPC, p2, (2/1 RPC, p4) twice.

Repeat rounds 1–16 for cable pattern.

YOKE

With longer circular needle, cast on 50 (50, 50, 54, 56, 58, 62, 64, 64) stitches.

Setup Row (WS): P2, place marker, p8 (8, 8, 10, 10, 10, 12, 12, 12), place marker, p30 (30, 30, 30, 32, 34, 34, 36, 36), place marker, p8 (8, 8, 10, 10, 10, 12, 12, 12), place marker, p2.

Raglan Inc Row (RS): *Knit to last stitch before marker, M1R, k1, slip marker, k1, M1L; repeat from * 3 more times, knit to end of row—58 (58, 58, 62, 64, 66, 70, 72, 72) stitches; 8 stitches increased.

Next row (WS): Purl.

Repeat these 2 rows 1 (1, 2, 2, 2, 2, 2, 2, 2) more time(s)—66 (66, 74, 78, 80, 82, 86, 88, 88) stitches.

Neck Inc Row (RS): K2, M1L, *knit to last stitch before marker, M1R, k1, slip marker, k1, M1L; repeat from * 3

more times, knit to last 2 stitches, M1R, k2—76 (76, 84, 88, 90, 92, 96, 98, 98) stitches; 10 stitches increased.

Work wrong-side row.

Repeat these 2 rows 7 (7, 7, 7, 8, 8, 8, 9, 9) more times—146 (146, 154, 158, 170, 172, 176, 188, 188) stitches.

Work right-side neck inc row.

Neck Inc Row (WS): P2, M1P, purl to last 2 stitches, M1P, p2—158 (158, 166, 170, 182, 184, 188, 200, 200) stitches; 2 stitches increased.

Repeat these 2 rows twice more—182 (182, 190, 194, 206, 208, 212, 224, 224) stitches.

Joining Row (RS): *Knit to last stitch before marker, M1R, k1, slip marker, k1, M1L; repeat from * 3 more times, knit to end of row, cast on 20 (20, 20, 20, 20, 22, 22, 22, 22) stitches using backward-loop cast-on, join to work in the round, knit 16 (16, 16, 16, 16, 15, 15, 15, 15) stitches, place marker for start of round—210 (210, 218, 222, 234, 238, 242, 254, 254) stitches.

Next rnd: Knit to last 52 stitches of round, work cable pattern.

Raglan Inc Rnd: *Knit to last stitch before marker, M1R, k1, slip marker, k1, M1L; repeat from * 3 more times, work in pattern to end of round—8 stitches increased.

Repeat these 2 rounds 4 (5, 5, 4, 4, 5, 4, 4, 3) more times—250 (258, 266, 262, 274, 286, 282, 294, 286) stitches total; 90 (92, 94, 92, 96, 100, 98, 102, 100) front stitches, 46 (48, 50, 50, 52, 54, 54, 56, 54) stitches each sleeve, 68 (70, 72, 70, 74, 78, 76, 80, 78) back stitches.

Next rnd: Work even in pattern.

SIZES – (35¾, 38½, 41¼, 44¼, 47, 50¾, 53½, 56½)" [– (91, 98, 105, 112.5, 119.5, 129, 136, 143.5)CM] ONLY
Body Inc Rnd: *Knit to last stitch before marker, M1R, k1, slip marker, knit to marker, slip marker, k1, M1L; repeat from * once more, work in pattern to end of round—4 stitches increased.

Next rnd: Work even in pattern.

Repeat these 2 rounds – (0, 2, 5, 6, 6, 9, 9, 10) more times for a total of – (262, 278, 286, 302, 314, 322, 334, 330) stitches; – (94, 100, 104, 110, 114, 118, 122, 122) front stitches, – (48, 50, 50, 52, 54, 54, 56, 54) stitches each sleeve, – (72, 78, 82, 88, 92, 96, 100, 100) back stitches.

All Sizes

Work 6 (6, 4, 2, 0, 0, 0, 0, 0) rounds even in pattern.

Sleeve Divide Rnd: *Work in pattern to marker, remove marker, slip 46 (48, 50, 50, 52, 54, 54, 56, 54) sleeve stitches onto waste yarn, cast on 1 (2, 2, 3, 3, 4, 6, 7, 10) stitch(es), place marker for side seam, cast on 1 (2, 2, 3, 3, 4, 6, 7, 10) stitch(es); repeat from * once, work in pattern to end of round, remove marker for start of round; left side seam marker will become start of round—162 (174, 186, 198, 210, 222, 238, 250, 262) stitches.

BODY

Work in pattern until body measures 2" (5cm) from underarm cast-on stitches or fullest bust point, ending with an odd-numbered round from cable pattern.

Short Row Bust Shaping

If the difference between your front and back length is less than 3" (7.5cm) omit bust shaping and move on to next section, All Sizes. Use bust shaping that corresponds to the difference between your front and back length; sizes S (M, L) are suitable for differences up to 4 (5, 6)" (10, 12.5, 15]cm).

Short Row 1 (RS): Work in pattern to 6 (8, 8, 9, 10, 12, 12, 14, 14) stitches past cable pattern, w&t.

Short Row 2 (WS): Work in pattern to 6 (8, 8, 9, 10, 12, 12, 14, 14) stitches past cable pattern, w&t.

SMALL
Short Row 3: Work in pattern to previously wrapped stitch, work wrap with stitch, work 1 (1, 2, 2, 3, 3, 3, 4, 4) stitch(es), w&t.

Work short row 3 nine more times.

MEDIUM
Short Row 3: Work in pattern to previously wrapped stitch, work wrap with stitch, work 0 (0, 1, 1, 1, 1, 2, 2, 2) stitch(es), w&t.

Work short row 3 fifteen more times.

LARGE
Short Row 3: Work in pattern to previously wrapped stitch, work wrap with stitch, work 0 (0, 0, 0, 0, 1, 1, 1, 1) stitch(es), w&t.

Work short row 3 twenty-one more times.

All Sizes
Work in pattern to end of round, working all wraps with the stitches they wrap as you pass.

Dart Placement Rnd: K23 (25, 27, 29, 31, 33, 36, 38, 40), place dart marker, k24 (26, 28, 30, 32, 34, 36, 38, 40), place dart marker, work to end of round.

Waist Dec Rnd: Knit to 2 stitches before dart marker, k2tog, slip marker, work to dart marker, slip marker, ssk, knit to 2 stitches before cable, k2tog, work cable pattern, ssk, knit to end of round—4 stitches decreased.

Work waist dec rnd every 7 (7, 7, 7, 8, 8, 9, 9, 9) rounds 4 more times—142 (154, 166, 178, 190, 202, 218, 230, 242) stitches.

Work 10 rounds even in pattern.

Hip Inc Rnd: Work to dart marker, M1R, slip marker, work to dart marker, slip marker, M1L, work to 1 stitch before cable, M1R, k1, work cable pattern, k1, M1L, knit to end of round—4 stitches increased.

Work hip inc rnd every 4 rounds 4 more times—162 (174, 186, 198, 210, 222, 238, 250, 262) stitches.

Remove dart markers.

Work even in pattern until desired length, finishing when cable pattern is complete.

Dec Rnd: Knit to cable, k2, p2, k2tog, k1, p2tog, p2tog, k2tog, k1, p2, k1, k2tog, p2tog, p1, k2tog, k1, p2, k1, ssk, p1, p2tog, k1, k2tog, p2, k1, ssk, p1, p2tog, k2tog, k1, p2, k1, k2tog, place marker for start of new round—148 (160, 172, 184, 196, 208, 224, 236, 248) stitches.

Ribbing Rnd: *P2, k2; repeat from * to end of round.

Work ribbing rnd until body measures 14½ (14½, 14½, 14½, 15, 15, 15, 15, 15)" (37 [37, 37, 37, 38, 38, 38, 38, 38]cm) from underarm or desired length, taking care to measure at side seam so short rows are not included.

Bind off all stitches in pattern.

SLEEVES

Starting at center of underarm cast-on stitches and using double-pointed needles, pick up and knit 1 (2, 2, 3, 3, 4, 6, 7, 10) stitch(es), place 46 (48, 50, 50, 52, 54, 54, 56, 54) stitches from waste yarn onto needle, knit these stitches, pick up and knit remaining 1 (2, 2, 3, 3, 4, 6, 7, 10) stitch(es) from underarm stitches, place marker for start of round—48 (52, 54, 56, 58, 62, 66, 70, 74) stitches.

Knit 19 (15, 12, 11, 10, 8, 8, 6, 6) rounds even.

Sleeve Dec Rnd: K1, k2tog, knit to last 3 stitches, ssk, k1—46 (50, 52, 54, 56, 60, 64, 68, 72); 2 stitches decreased.

Work these 20 (16, 13, 12, 11, 9, 9, 7, 7) rounds 3 (5, 6, 7, 8, 10, 10, 12, 14) more times—40 (40, 40, 40, 40, 40, 44, 44, 44) stitches.

Work even until sleeve measures 16 (16½, 16½, 16½, 17, 17, 17, 17½, 17½)" (40.5 [42, 42, 42, 43, 43, 43, 44.5, 44.5]cm) from underarm.

Ribbing Rnd: *P2, k2; repeat from * to end of round.

Work ribbing rnd until cuff measures 2" (5cm) or desired length. Bind off all stitches in pattern.

Repeat for second sleeve.

FINISHING

Cowl Neck

Using small circular needle and starting at the right side of the neck cast-on stitches, pick up and knit 50 (50, 50, 54, 56, 58, 62, 64, 64) cast-on stitches, pick up and knit 19 (19, 21, 21, 22, 22, 22, 25, 25) stitches to edge of front cast-on, pick up and knit 20 (20, 20, 20, 20, 22, 22, 22, 22) cast-on stitches, pick up and knit 19 (19, 21, 21, 22, 22, 22, 25, 25) stitches to complete round, place marker,

join to work in round—108 (108, 112, 116, 120, 124, 128, 136, 136) stitches.

Ribbing Rnd: *K2, p2; repeat from * to end of round.

Work ribbing rnd until cowl measures 8" (20.5cm) or desired length. Bind off all stitches in pattern.

Weave in all loose ends. Block garment to dimensions given on schematic.

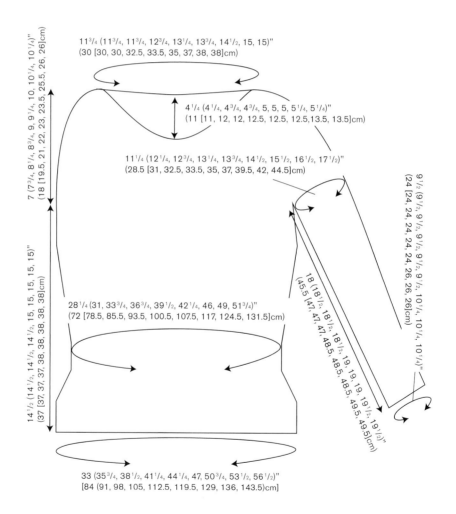

11³/₄ (11³/₄, 11³/₄, 12³/₄, 13¹/₄, 13³/₄, 14¹/₂, 15, 15)"
(30 [30, 30, 32.5, 33.5, 35, 37, 38, 38]cm)

7 (7³/₄, 8¹/₄, 8³/₄, 9, 9¹/₄, 10, 10¹/₄, 10¹/₄)"
(18 [19.5, 21, 22, 23, 23.5, 25.5, 26, 26]cm)

4¹/₄ (4¹/₄, 4³/₄, 4³/₄, 5, 5, 5, 5¹/₄, 5¹/₄)"
(11 [11, 12, 12, 12.5, 12.5, 12.5, 13.5, 13.5]cm)

11¹/₄ (12¹/₄, 12³/₄, 13¹/₄, 13³/₄, 14¹/₂, 15¹/₂, 16¹/₂, 17¹/₂)"
(28.5 [31, 32.5, 33.5, 35, 37, 39.5, 42, 44.5]cm)

9¹/₂ (9¹/₂, 9¹/₂, 9¹/₂, 9¹/₂, 9¹/₂, 10¹/₄, 10¹/₄, 10¹/₄)"
(24 [24, 24, 24, 24, 24, 26, 26, 26]cm)

14¹/₂ (14¹/₂, 14¹/₂, 14¹/₂, 15, 15, 15, 15, 15)"
(37 [37, 37, 37, 38, 38, 38, 38, 38]cm)

28¹/₄ (31, 33³/₄, 36³/₄, 39¹/₂, 42¹/₄, 46, 49, 51³/₄)"
(72 [78.5, 85.5, 93.5, 100.5, 107.5, 117, 124.5, 131.5]cm)

18 (18¹/₂, 18¹/₂, 18¹/₂, 19, 19, 19, 19¹/₂, 19¹/₂)"
(45.5 [47, 47, 47, 48.5, 48.5, 48.5, 49.5, 49.5]cm)

33 (35³/₄, 38¹/₂, 41¹/₄, 44¹/₄, 47, 50³/₄, 53¹/₂, 56¹/₂)"
[84 (91, 98, 105, 112.5, 119.5, 129, 136, 143.5)cm]

Note: Cowl and short row bust shaping are not shown on the schematic.

ACKNOWLEDGMENTS

Every book feels like a journey: You start with great expectation and excitement, then comes the hard slog—and often exhaustion and frustration—before you finally get to the end of the journey and the joy and satisfaction of a beautiful finished book.

I have so many people to thank:

* my husband, Joseph, who encouraged and organized me, as well as photographing the projects beautifully. It wouldn't have happened without him.
* my parents, who have supported me every step along the way.
* my sons, Caelen, Damien, Dylan, and Lucas, who each provide me with constant inspiration and purpose.
* an extra thanks to Caelen, for his excellent Illustrator work.
* my dedicated technical editor, Heather Murray, who debated the finer technical points with me.
* my sample knitters, Eimear Earley, Kathy Kyburz, and Aine Riordan, who created beautiful projects and helped the book finish on time.
* my test knitters, Kelly Ashfield, Jeannie-Maree Becker, Daniela Bevilacqua, Debbie Chase, Sue Cullen, Ursa Hawthorne, Holly Jackson, Sheila Jones, Erin Mahoney, Bonnie Politano, and Mairead Quinn, who made sure my directions made sense.
* my models, Ada Cunningham, Caelen Feller, Ciara Murphy, Clare Murphy, Charlotte Punter, Jordon Walshe, and Alice Webb.
* the editorial, creative, and production teams at Potter Craft, who got the book to the finish line, specifically Angelin Borsics, Caitlin Harpin, Michael Nagin, Stephanie Huntwork, Patricia Shaw, La Tricia Watford, and Heather Williamson.

And, finally, thanks to the many suppliers, listed in the back of this book, who provided the yarn and buttons, without which the projects would not have been knit!

STANDARD YARN WEIGHT SYSTEM

CYCA	0	1	2	3	4	5	6
Type of Yarns in Category	Fingering, 10-count crochet thread	Sock, Fingering, Baby	Sport, Baby	DK, Light Worsted	Worsted, Afghan, Aran	Chunky, Craft, Rug	Bulky, Roving
Knit Gauge Range* in Stockinette Stitch to 4" (10cm)	33–40† sts	27–32 sts	23–26 sts	21–24 sts	16–20 sts	12–15 sts	6–11 sts
Recommended Needle in US Size Range	000–1	1–3	3–5	5–7	7–9	9–11	11 and larger
Recommended Needle in Metric Size Range	1.5–2.25mm	2.25–3.25mm	3.25–3.75mm	3.75–4.5mm	4.5–5.5mm	5.5–8mm	8mm and larger

* *Guidelines only:* The above information reflects the most commonly used gauges and needle sizes for specific yarn categories.

† Laceweight yarns are usually knitted on larger needles to create lacy, openwork patterns. Accordingly, a gauge range is difficult to determine. Always follow the gauge stated in the pattern.

RESOURCES

Yarn and buttons were kindly provided by the following companies. Most of the yarn (or a suitable substitute) should be available from your local yarn store. If you are substituting yarn, use the yarn weight system (page 153) and the fiber type to find a good alternative.

YARN

ANZULA LUXURY FIBERS
740 H St.
Fresno, CA 93721
www.anzula.com

BARE NAKED YARNS
1508 Harvard Ave. NW
Canton, OH 44703
www.knitspot.com

BERROCO, INC.
1 Tupperware Dr., Suite 4
N. Smithfield, RI 02896-6815
(401) 769-1212
www.berroco.com

BLUE MOON FIBERS, INC.
56587 Mollenhour Rd.
Scappoose, OR 97056
www.bluemoonfiberarts.com

CASCADE YARNS
PO Box 58168
Tukwila, WA 98138
(800) 548-1048
www.cascadeyarns.com

FYBERSPATES LTD.
16 Northgate
Utkinton, Tarporley
Cheshire CW6 0LL
UK
01829 732525
www.fyberspates.co.uk

GREEN MOUNTAIN SPINNERY
PO Box 568
Putney, VT 05346-0568
(802) 387-4528
www.spinnery.com

HARRISVILLE TWEED
PO Box 806
Harrisville, NH 03450
(800) 338-9415
www.harrisville.com

HEDGEHOG FIBRES
612 Harbour Point
Little Island
Cork, Ireland
www.hedgehogfibres.com

LORNA'S LACES
4229 N. Honore St.
Chicago, IL 60613
(773) 935-3803
www.lornaslaces.net

MALABRIGO
US: (786) 866-6187
Europe, UK: 44 20 3318 5173
www.malabrigoyarn.com

MANOS DEL URUGUAY
www.fairmountfibers.com
www.artesanoyarns.co.uk

MISS BABS
PO Box 78
Mountain City, TN 37683
(423) 727-0670
www.missbabs.com

NORO
PO Box 336
315 Bayview Ave.
Amityville, NY 11701
www.knittingfever.com
www.designeryarns.uk.com

O-WOOL CLASSIC
915 N. 28th St.
Philadelphia, PA 19130
(888) 673-0260
www.o-wool.com

SHIBUI KNITS
1500 N.W. 18th, Suite 110
Portland, OR 97209
(503) 595-5898
www.shibuiknits.com

SKACEL COLLECTION, INC.
Seattle, WA
US: (800) 255-1278
Canada: (866) 966-5945
www.skacelknitting.com

SWEET GEORGIA YARNS
10-408 E. Kent Ave. South
Vancouver, BC V5X 2X7
Canada
(604) 569-6811
www.sweetgeorgiayarns.com

BUTTONS

Textile Garden
Unit 5, Annington Commercial Centre
Annington Rd.
Steyning BN44 3WA
UK
44 1903 815702; 44 7736 904109
www.textilegarden.com

GENERAL TECHNIQUES

Any special cast-on, bind-off, or seaming techniques used in the patterns for this book are fully detailed either here or within the pattern.

Cast-On Techniques

Backward-Loop Cast-On

Begin by placing a slip knot on the needle. *Twist a loop of the working yarn backward in the yarn, place the loop on the needle, and pull the working yarn to tighten the stitch up; repeat from * until the desired number of stitches have been cast on.

Cable Cast-On

If there are no stitches on the needle, create slip knot, knit into slip knot, place stitch created from right to left needle. *Knit into the gap between the first 2 stitches, slip new stitch created from right to left needle; repeat from * until desired number of stitches have been cast on. If you are casting on with stitches already on the needle, you can begin at *.

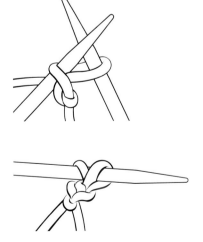

Knitted Cast-On

If there are no stitches on the needle, create a slip knot, knit into the slip knot, place the stitch created from right to left needle. *Knit into the first stitch, slip the new stitch created from right to left needle; repeat from * until the desired number of stitches have been cast on. If you are casting on with stitches already on the needle, you can begin at *.

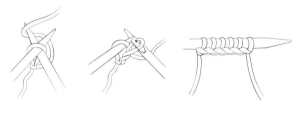

Long-Tail Cast-On

When a cast-on type is not specified, this is the basic one that I use in my patterns.

Begin by leaving a long tail, typically, three times the length of the cast-on you are working. This cast-on uses only one needle held in front of you.

1. Create a slip knot and tighten it onto your needle. Keep your working yarn to your right and your yarn tail to your left.

2. With your left thumb, create a loop in the yarn tail and hold your index finger in front of the working yarn. Grip the end of both yarns with your other fingers.

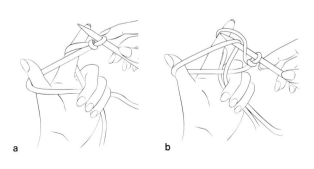

a   b

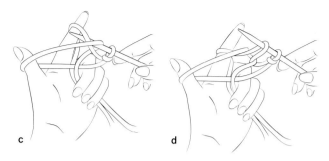

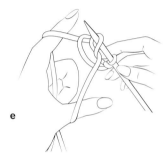

3. From bottom to top, pull the needle through the yarn loop on your thumb.

4. Lift the needle up to your index finger and pull the yarn through from right to left.

5. Dropping the loop off your thumb, tighten both ends of the yarn until you are happy with the tension of the stitch.

6. Repeat steps 2 to 4 until you have the correct number of stitches on the needle.

Provisional Cast-On (Crochet Method)

This cast-on method uses waste yarn and a crochet hook to create a crochet chain that wraps a stitch around your knitting needle at the same time. It is not necessary to know how to crochet to use this method.

1. Make a slip knot with waste yarn and place it on the crochet hook.

2. Hold the crochet hook above the needle, *wrap the yarn around under the needle and then wrap yarn over crochet hook and pull through the stitch on the hook.* There is 1 stitch on the needle and 1 stitch on the hook.

3. Repeat from * to * until you have the appropriate number of stitches on the needle.

4. When you have cast on the correct number of stitches, pull the end of the yarn through the final stitch on the crochet hook and put a knot at the end of the yarn to mark the side where you will begin unraveling the crochet chain.

5. Switch to the project yarn and begin knitting.

When you need to remove the provisional cast-on, unravel the crochet chain, starting at the knotted end. Carefully place each of the live stitches exposed on a needle and begin working as instructed.

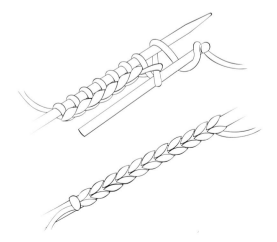

Bind-Off Techniques
Elastic Bind-Off

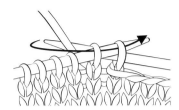

K1, *k1, slip 2 stitches to the left needle, knit 2 stitches together through their back loops; repeat from * to the end.

Note: This assumes all stitches are knit; if you are working with a purl stitch, substitute *purl* for *knit* in the directions.

I-Cord Bind-Off

Cast on 3 stitches at the start of the row, *k2, ssk, place all 3 stitches back on the left needle and repeat from * until all stitches have been worked. With 3 I-cord stitches remaining on the needle, k3tog, break yarn, and draw through the final stitch.

Three-Needle Bind-Off

With right sides of both pieces together, hold the two needles parallel in your left hand, with the wrong side facing you. *Insert the third needle into the first stitch on the front needle and the first stitch on the back needle. Knit these 2 stitches together. Repeat from *, then pass the outer stitch on the right needle over the stitch just made to bind off. Continue from * until all stitches have been bound off. Cut yarn and pull the tail through the last stitch to secure.

Grafting (Kitchener Stitch)

Place an equal number of stitches on the front and back needles; break the yarn, leaving a generous tail. Thread a tapestry needle with the yarn.

1. Pull needle through first front stitch as if to purl.

2. Pull needle through first back stitch as if to knit.

3. Pull needle through first front stitch as if to knit and slip stitch off needle. Pull needle through next front stitch as if to purl but leave stitch on needle.

4. Pull needle through first back stitch as if to purl and slip stitch off needle. Pull needle through next back stitch as if to knit but leave stitch on needle.

Repeat steps 3 and 4 until all stitches have been worked. Take care to pull yarn carefully through worked stitches periodically. Make sure you do not work it too tightly, as it should look like a knitted stitch.

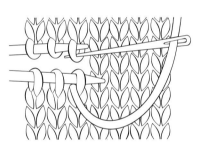

Common Stitch Patterns
Garter Stitch

When working flat, knit every row (WS and RS). If working in the round, knit all odd-numbered rounds and purl all even-numbered rounds.

Stockinette Stitch

When working flat, knit every RS row and purl every WS row. If working in the round, knit all rounds (RS).

Reverse Stockinette Stitch

When working flat, purl every RS row and knit every WS row. If working in the round, purl all rounds (RS).

ABBREVIATIONS

*	repeat instructions from asterisk as indicated	m	meter(s)
"	inch(es)	MC	main color
CC	contrasting color	mm	millimeter(s)
cm	centimeter(s)	p	purl
dec	decrease(ing)	p2tog	purl 2 stitches together
g	grams	RS	right side(s)
inc	increase(ing)	rnd(s)	round(s)
k	knit	ssk	slip 2 stitches individually as if to knit, then knit those 2 stitches together through the back loops (left-slanting decrease)
kfb	knit into the front and back of one stitch—increases 1 stitch		
k2tog	knit 2 together (right-slanting decrease)	sssk	slip 3 stitches individually as if to knit, then knit those 3 stitches together through the back loops (left-slanting decrease)
k3tog	knit 3 stitches together		
M1R	Insert left needle, from back to front, under strand of yarn that runs between next stitch on left needle and last stitch on right needle; knit this loop through the front.	ssp	slip 2 stitches individually as if to knit, then purl those 2 stitches together through the back loops
		sssp	slip 3 stitches individually as if to knit, then purl those 3 stitches together through the back loops
M1P	Insert left needle, from back to front, under strand of yarn that runs between next stitch on left needle and last stitch on right needle; purl this stitch.	st(s)	stitch(es)
		tbl	through back loop
		WS	wrong side(s)
M1L	Insert left needle, from front to back, under strand of yarn that runs between next stitch on left needle and last stitch on right needle; knit this loop through the back.	w&t	wrap and turn (short row)
		yd	yard(s)
		yo	yarn over
M2	Insert left needle, from back to front, under strand of yarn that runs between next stitch on left needle and last stitch on right needle; knit front of this stitch and then knit back of stitch.		

INDEX (Page references in *italics* refer to illustrations.)